THE HIDDEN TREASURE THAT LIES IN PLAIN SIGHT 4

The Day of the Lord and the End of America

JEREMY SHORTER
www.jeremyshorter.net

authorHOUSE®

AuthorHouse™
1663 Liberty Drive
Bloomington, IN 47403
www.authorhouse.com
Phone: 1 (800) 839-8640

Published by AuthorHouse 04/09/2018

ISBN: 978-1-5246-7362-8 (sc)
ISBN: 978-1-5246-7363-5 (e)

Library of Congress Control Number: 2017903423

Print information available on the last page.

This book is printed on acid-free paper.

Thank You for buying my Book. If you like this Book you will also like the rest of my Books. Feel free to email or call me anytime with questions, Thank you again for purchasing this Book. If you found that this book as help you please leave an honest review on Amazon Barns & Noble or any other site that you purchased the book from.

To purchase more of my Books visit

www.JeremyShorter.net

Contents

Foreword

By Adolf Hitler

"The day mankind finds out what I was trying to defend this nation, Germany, from then that's the day World War 3 will start. **For on that day, mankind will learn that I was trying to save my nation from The Free Masons, the Illuminati, the Jews.** For if the Americans wins the war, they will conquer the world and forever be a slave to the Jews and they will try to conquer God. Do you know who America has in it's possessions? "NO," the solider replied.

The Americans have the jewels of God. The Americans have stolen God's precious jewels. "What do you mean his precocious jewels?" THE SOLDIER asked. Hitler said, **"America has stolen the Jews. The Jews of God. His jewelry. The Negroes. They are the true Hebrews**. What a foolish move and a direct challenge to God. **And they plan on moving these false white Jews into a state of Israel.** America is desperate in it's attempt to win this war using atom bombs on Japan. America will destroy the whole world in it's attempt to conquer it.

When America its Jewish Slave masters conquer the world and the world realize I was right, then all the nations will begin a third world war to dethrone America of it's rule. Every nation will soon posses atom bombs of their own. It will be the end of the world as we know it.

"Why will the Jews control America? The solider asked.

Hitler said, "**because the white Jews knows that the Negroes are the real children of Israel and to keep Americas secret the Jews will blackmail America.** The will extort America, **their plan for world domination won't work if the Negroes know who they were**. The white citizens of America will be terrified to know that all this time they've been mistreating and discriminating and lynching the children of Israel. They will fear God will destroy them as he destroyed Egypt for doing the same thing. **So the Elite, the Illuminati keeps this a secret at all cost**. After I die I will one day cause World War 3 just by this message which will be like planting a seed in a people minds until it sprouts once they nurture that seed and seek more truth and learn Hitler was right. **I did the world a favor by killing the false Jews before they designated a false state of Israel**. But I fear I have failed. The world will fall into the hands of Satan.

Adolf Hitler
A German Politician

Preface

This book gives biblical and historical information about the Biblical Hebrew Israelites (children of Israel/12 Tribes). In this book, I would like to shed light on the End of America and the Day of the Lord and much more. My prayer and hope are that my work that I do for the Most High God can inspire and encourage others to serve the Most High God, and to do his will.

2 Esdras 8:1 And he answered me, saying, The most High hath made this world for many, but the world to come for few. – *Authorized KJV Apocrypha*

★ 1 ★

The Bible: A History Book of the So-Called Negros and the 12 Tribes

Introduction

The Bible is a history book of the original black Hebrew Israelites and the 12 Tribes who are the children of Israel. Throughout history, they show the white European civilization as the first civilization. History has been handed down to the so called Negros (Hebrew Israelites) by false pictures of human history altered history and the cover-up of the truth. One who is well learned in Ancient History will be able to see past the lies and see the truth to which Nationality of people the bible refers to.

The Bible gives reliable evidence of the History of the Black Hebrew Israelites and the 12 Tribes. The bible itself is a mystery book full of prophecies and future prophecies of the people mentioned in the book. Biblical history has shown that the children of Israel (Hebrew Israelites) are spread throughout the world. What we must understand is that the so-called Negros (Hebrew Israelites) people wrote the Bible and they wrote it showing their history culture, mission, and their connection with the Creator (The Most High). I must also point out that the Hebrew Israelites are the original Jews. The ancient Biblical definition of the word "Jew" is a member of the tribe of Judah name of Jacob's fourth son. World English Dictionary defines Jew as "a member of the Semitic people who claim descent from the ancient Hebrew who is referred to as "Jews" one must engage in an in-depth study of the Bible and research history.

Because of their disobedient not keeping the laws and statutes of the Most High they fell as a nation and were dispersed throughout the four corners of the world. This ultimately caused them to forget their heritage as a Great people. As you keep reading the book, I will discuss the color of the Hebrew Israelites and their duty as the Most High chosen people.

★2★

Day of the Lord

Most people associate the day of the Lord with a period of time or a special day that will occur when God's will and purpose for His world and for mankind will be fulfilled. Some scholars believe that the day of the Lord will be a longer period of time than a single day and period of time when Christ will reign throughout the world before He cleanses heaven and earth in preparation for the eternal state of all mankind. The day of the Lord is a day of greater trouble which The Most High God will heap upon all those who are upon the Earth. Let us fast, pray and get ourselves together spiritually at this present time.

> **Joel 1:15 Alas for the day! for the day of the LORD is at hand, and as a destruction from the Almighty shall it come.**

The day of the Lord is a day of darkness, not happiness as the church makes it out to be. It's a time of exceeding great troubles and calamities. That's why it's important to be doing the will of the Most High God and staying in scripture

Joel 2:2 A day of darkness and of gloominess, a day of clouds and of thick darkness, as the morning spread upon the mountains: a great people and a strong; there hath not been ever the like, neither shall be any more after it, even to the years of many generations.

Gloominess - Causing gloom; dismal or depressing sad; sadden.

The day of the Lord will be very terrible, so my question is this: Why do the majority of the churches (congregation) teach that everything is going to be alright and that you will be raptured off? All these are doctrines of men, be not deceived.

Joel 2:11 And the LORD shall utter his voice before his army: for his camp is very great: for he is strong that executeth his word: for the day of the LORD is great and very terrible; and who can abide it?

The day of the Lord is a day of destruction, not happiness.

Isaiah 13:6-13 Howl ye; for the day of the LORD is at hand; it shall come as a destruction from the Almighty.

7 Therefore shall all hands be faint, and every man's heart shall melt:

8 And they shall be afraid: pangs and sorrows shall take hold of them; they shall be in pain as a woman that travaileth: they shall be amazed one at another; their faces shall be as flames.

9 Behold, the day of the LORD cometh, cruel both with wrath and fierce anger, to lay the land desolate: and he shall destroy the sinners thereof out of it.

10 For the stars of heaven and the constellations thereof shall not give their light: the sun shall be

darkened in his going forth, and the moon shall not cause her light to shine.

11 And I will punish the world for their evil, and the wicked for their iniquity; and I will cause the arrogancy of the proud to cease, and will lay low the haughtiness of the terrible.

12 I will make a man more precious than fine gold; even a man than the golden wedge of Ophir.

13 Therefore I will shake the heavens, and the earth shall remove out of her place, in the wrath of the LORD of hosts, and in the day of his fierce anger.

The day of the Lord shall have no light in it, it shall be very dark.

Amos 5:18-20 Woe unto you that desire the day of the LORD! to what end is it for you? the day of the LORD is darkness and not light.

19 As if a man did flee from a lion, and a bear met him; or went into the house, and leaned his hand on the wall, and a serpent bit him.

20 Shall not the day of the LORD be darkness, and not light? even very dark, and no brightness in it?

What will people be doing when Christ return?

The scripture tells us when the Son of Man (Christ/Messiah) returns, people will be eating drinking marrying and given in marriage, meaning fathers will be giving their daughters over to marriage. People will not observe the time in which Christ shall return. These are the last days we are living in. So let us stay focus on the Most High God of Israel and repent.

Luke 17:26-30 And as it was in the days of Noe, so shall it be also in the days of the Son of man.

27 They did eat, they drank, they married wives, they were given in marriage, until the day that Noe entered into the ark, and the flood came, and destroyed them all.

28 Likewise also as it was in the days of Lot; they did eat, they drank, they bought, they sold, they planted, they builded;

29 But the same day that Lot went out of Sodom it rained fire and brimstone from heaven, and destroyed them all.

30 Even thus shall it be in the day when the Son of man is revealed.

Will you know the day and hour of Christ return?

We will not know that day or hour. The Messiah will come as a thief in the night. That's why it's important to be doing the will of the Most High God, so you can store up good works.

2 Peter 3:9-10 The Lord is not slack concerning his promise, as some men count slackness; but is longsuffering to us-ward, not willing that any should perish, but that all should come to repentance.

10 But the day of the Lord will come as a thief in the night; in the which the heavens shall pass away with a great noise, and the elements shall melt with fervent heat, the earth also and the works that are therein shall be burned up.

The scriptures tell us to be as a watchman waiting on a thief, likewise we are to be like that waiting of the Son of Man (Christ) at an hour that we know not.

Luke 12:39-40 And this know, that if the goodman of the house had known what hour the thief would come, he would have watched, and not have suffered his house to be broken through.

40 Be ye therefore ready also: for the Son of man cometh at an hour when ye think not.

Only the Most High God knows the day that the Son of Man will come.

Matthew 24:36 But of that day and hour knoweth no man, no, not the angels of heaven, but my Father only.

What can you do to prepare yourself for Christ return?

We are to be watchful and always in prayer that we may be accounted worthy to escape all the evil in these last day.

Luke 21:34-36 And take heed to yourselves, lest at any time your hearts be overcharged with surfeiting, and drunkenness, and cares of this life, and so that day come upon you unawares.

35 For as a snare shall it come on all them that dwell on the face of the whole earth.

36 Watch ye therefore, and pray always, that ye may be accounted worthy to escape all these things that shall come to pass, and to stand before the Son of man.

Let us put on the whole armor of the Most High God that we are able to stand against the wiles of the devil in these last days and while serving the Most High God.

Ephesians 6:11-12 Put on the whole armour of God, that ye may be able to stand against the wiles of the devil.

12 For we wrestle not against flesh and blood, but against principalities, against powers, against the rulers of the darkness of this world, against spiritual wickedness in high places.

13 Wherefore take unto you the whole armour of God, that ye may be able to withstand in the evil day, and having done all, to stand.

Let us stay in prayer day and night. Let the Most High God hear our prayers continuously in these last days. Let us be found worthy to be saved. We are to be praying without ceasing (no stop).

1 Thessalonians 5:17 Pray without ceasing.

Conclusion

Besides being a time of judgment, it will also be a time of salvation as God will deliver the remnant of Israel, fulfilling His promise that "all of Israel will be saved" (Romans 11:26), forgiving their sins and restoring His chosen people to the land He promised to Abraham (Isaiah 10:27; Jeremiah 30:19-31, 40; Micah 4; Zechariah 13). Let us stay focus pray and always be watchful, for these are truly the last days.

Revelation 19:11 And I saw heaven opened, and behold a white horse; and he that sat upon him was called Faithful and True, and in righteousness he doth judge and make war.

★ 3 ★

End of America

America as we know it is heading towards a dark path in fact it as always had a dark path. America is spiritual Babylon according the word of the Most High God. In Revelation Chapter 17-18, it talks about the destruction of Babylon. America is falling due to its sins and the Most High God judgement is upon America and wherever the Most High God people are. America is very prideful and wicked and has shed innocent blood. America doesn't believe in the Most High God, satan is their god aswell as other nations.

Obadia 1:3-4 The pride of thine heart hath deceived thee, thou that dwellest in the clefts of the rock, Whose habitation is high; that saith in his heart, Who shall bring me down to the ground?

4 Though thou exalt thyself as the eagle, and though thou set thy nest among the stars, thence will I bring thee down, saith the Lord.

Flee America

We must understand and know that America was never our (12 Tribes) resting place. The so called Negros and some of the other 12 Tribes was brought over to America (Deuteronomy 28:65) to serve their captivity, because they disobeyed the Most High God word. I will talk later in the book about this. Ask yourself, why would one stay in a place that is falling? They have brainwashed the people in America to make them believe that other places are nasty and or not good living conditions. Fact, one can live easier outside of America than in America at this present time. America is the Great Whore.

Revelation 18:4 And I heard another voice from heaven, saying, Come out of her, my people, that ye be not partakers of her sins, and that ye receive not of her plagues.

Partakers - to take or have a part in; share.

The Most High God has spread the 12 Tribes throughout the four corners of the World due to their disobedient. It will be a time when The Most High God will call them back to their land. For he (The God of Israel) will deliver them from the four corners of the World and bring them back to their land which he have given them. The Most High God said flee from the land of the north, that's North America.

Zechariah 2:6-8 Ho, ho, come forth, and flee from the land of the north, saith the LORD: for I have spread you abroad as the four winds of the heaven, saith the LORD.

7 Deliver thyself, O Zion, that dwellest with the daughter of Babylon.

8 For thus saith the LORD of hosts; After the glory hath he sent me unto the nations which spoiled you: for he that toucheth you toucheth the apple of his eye.

Flee - to run away, as from danger or pursuers; take flight.

America has sinned so much that it has reached unto heaven. America is the habitation of devils. The Most High God will punish America which is Babylon. The Most High God will reward her (America) double for all the things she has done to the Most High God people (12 Tribes) and other countries, like going to war for oil slavery the killing of the North American Indians who are from the tribe of Gad (12 Tribes), and much more.

> **Revelation 18:5-7 For her sins have reached unto heaven, and God hath remembered her iniquities.**
>
> **6 Reward her even as she rewarded you, and double unto her double according to her works: in the cup which she hath filled fill to her double.**
>
> **7 How much she hath glorified herself, and lived deliciously, so much torment and sorrow give her: for she saith in her heart, I sit a queen, and am no widow, and shall see no sorrow.**

The Judgment of America

Judgment is upon America (Babylon) as we know it, and America will be destroyed by fire and nuclear bombs. The word of the Most High God has already declared it.

> **Jeremiah 50:14-15 Put yourselves in array against Babylon round about: all ye that bend the bow, shoot at her, spare no arrows: for she hath sinned against the LORD.**
>
> **15 Shout against her round about: she hath given her hand: her foundations are fallen, her walls are thrown down: for it is the vengeance of the LORD: take vengeance upon her; as she hath done, do unto her.**

America plagues shall come in one day death, and mourning, and famine and She (America) shall be burned with fire for that is the judgement of America.

Revelation 18:8 Therefore shall her plagues come in one day, death, and mourning, and famine; and she shall be utterly burned with fire: for strong is the Lord God who judgeth her.

Death - the act of dying; the end of life; the total and permanent cessation of all the vital functions of an organism.

Plagues - Any widespread affliction, calamity, or evil, esp. one regarded as a direct punishment by God.

Mourning - The act of a person who mourns; sorrowing or lamentation.

Famine - extreme and general scarcity of food, as in a country or a large geographical area.

America has made other Country Kings rich and they have lived deliciously off her and committed fornication with her. They shall cry for the destruction of America when they see the smoke from her (America) burring from their country. They will see America be destroyed in one hour.

Revelation 18:9-10 And the kings of the earth, who have committed fornication and lived deliciously with her, shall bewail her, and lament for her, when they shall see the smoke of her burning,

10 Standing afar off for the fear of her torment, saying, Alas, alas, that great city Babylon, that mighty city! for in one hour is thy judgment come.

Bewail - to express great sorrow over (a person or thing); lament.

★4★

Escape within the Borders

As we read in the previous chapter that America (Babylon) will be judge by the Most High God, and he is telling his people (12 Tribes) to flee escape from that wicked place. The Most High God has an appointed area for safety when Armageddon starts and that's within his borders. You will read later on in this chapter about the borders of the Most High God. His borders are in the East; likewise the Son of Man (Christ/Messiah) will come from the east. This can be pointed out in the following scripture:

> **Matthew 24:27 For as the lightning cometh out of the east, and shineth even unto the west; so shall also the coming of the Son of man be.**

A Remnant will be saved

A Remnant of Israel (12 Tribes) will be saved. Not everybody in Israel will be saved only a remnant. If it's the Most High god will for you to escape within the Most High God Borders.

Romans 9:27 Esaias also crieth concerning Israel, Though the number of the children of Israel be as the sand of the sea, a remnant shall be saved:

Remnant - **1**. a fragment or scrap.
2. a remaining, usually small part, quantity, number.
3. remaining; left over.
4. a surviving trace or vestige.

Only a tenth shall return out of Israel (12 Tribes). A small remnant reserved, that number being put indefinitely.

Isaiah 6:13 But yet in it shall be a tenth, and it shall return, and shall be eaten: as a teil tree, and as an oak, whose substance is in them, when they cast their leaves: so the holy seed shall be the substance thereof.

In Isaiah 10:20 it's says a remnant of Israel shall be saved, these are those who escape out of the house of Jacob (Israel / 12 Tribes). Noticed it said those who have escaped. Only a remnant shall be saved for the elect of the Most High God. This remnant will remember who they are they will strive to keep the Laws statues and commandments of the Most High God.

Isaiah 10:20-22 And it shall come to pass in that day, that the remnant of Israel, and such as are escaped of the house of Jacob, shall no more again stay upon him that smote them; but shall stay upon the Most High, the Holy One of Israel, in truth.

21 The remnant shall return, even the remnant of Jacob, unto the mighty God.

22 For though thy people Israel be as the sand of the sea, yet a remnant of them shall return: the consumption decreed shall overflow with righteousness.

Gathering of his People

The Most High God of Israel is going to gather his people again for the second time and last time to save that remnant that is to be saved. The first time when the Children of Israel was saved was when they were in Egypt and the Most High God parted the Red Sea by the hand of Moses that can be pointed out in Exodus chapter 14. The Most High God will gather his people (12 Tribes) in the last days because he scattered them due to them disobedient to him, thus placing them in a 400 year curse. That's why it's important to flee America and get within the borders of the Most High God.

> **Isaiah 11:11 And it shall come to pass in that day, that the Most High shall set his hand again the second time to recover the remnant of his people, which shall be left, from Assyria, and from Egypt, and from Pathros, and from Cush, and from Elam, and from Shinar, and from Hamath, and from the islands of the sea.**

The Borders of God

The Borders of The Most High God is the land that he promised Abraham that he would give unto his seed. And that land is from the river of Egypt unto the great river, the river of Euphrates.

> **Genesis 15:18-21 In the same day the LORD made a covenant with Abram, saying, Unto thy seed have I given this land, from the river of Egypt unto the great river, the river Euphrates:**
>
> **19 The Kenites, and the Kenizzites, and the Kadmonites,**
>
> **20 And the Hittites, and the Perizzites, and the Rephaims,**

21 And the Amorites, and the Canaanites, and the Girgashites, and the Jebusites.

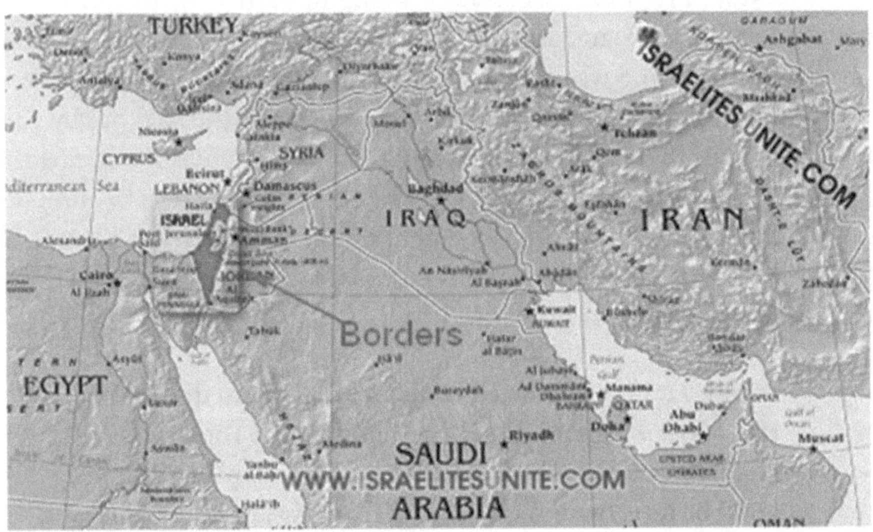

Those that escape all the said things in Matthew 24 shall escape by their works and faith. As the scriptures has said faith without work is dead, but those who have works and faith will escape, because they believe in the Most High God. The Most High God said they will see his salvation from his land, and within his borders. They are the remnant that has already been sanctified by the Most High God form the beginning of their creation.

2 Esdras 9:7-8 And every one that shall be saved, and shall be able to escape by his works, and by faith, whereby ye have believed,

8 Shall be preserved from the said perils, and shall see my salvation in my land, and within my borders: for I have sanctified them for me from the beginning. – *Authorized KJV Apocrypha*

Those who have already been pressed upon his borders shall he deliver with mercy.

2 Esdras 12:34 For the rest of my people shall he deliver with mercy, those that have been pressed upon my borders, and he shall make them joyful until the coming of the day of judgment, whereof I have spoken unto thee from the beginning. – *Authorized KJV Apocrypha*

Conclusion

Let us watch and pray always that we may be accounted worthy to stand before the Son of Man (Christ). If you are left in America or anywhere else, don't accept the mark of the beast mentioned in Revelation chapter 13. Let us humble ourselves and serve the Most High God in fear and obey his Words for they are faithful and true.

Luke 21:36 Watch ye therefore, and pray always, that ye may be accounted worthy to escape all these things that shall come to pass, and to stand before the Son of man.

★ 5 ★

True Names

Many of us don't know the father true name or the Messiah true name. We have to understand we have been given Greek gods names like Yhwh, Yahweh, Jesus, God, Jehovah and ect in-replace of the true names AHAYAH ASHAR AHAYAH (I AM THAT I AM) and YASHAYA (Christ). Hebrew is the Original Language. In the book of Jubilees one of the many books that were revealed to Moses during his 40 days and 40 nights on Mount Sinai (2 Edras 14:1-6). Moses was commanded to reveal some things; and some things were to be hidden. The "secrets of times" in 2 Edras 14 is a direct reference to the book of Jubilees. Please see below for scripture reference:

> **2 Esdras 14:1-6 And it came to pass upon the third day, I sat under an oak, and, behold, there came a voice out of a bush over against me, and said, Esdras, Esdras.**
>
> **2 And I said, Here am I, Lord And I stood up upon my feet.**

3 Then said he unto me, In the bush I did manifestly reveal myself unto Moses, and talked with him, when my people served in Egypt:

4 And I sent him and led my people out of Egypt, and brought him up to the mount of where I held him by me a long season,

5 And told him many wondrous things, and shewed him the secrets of the times, and the end; and commanded him, saying,

6 These words shalt thou declare, and these shalt thou hide. – *Authorized KJV Apocrypha*

As I mentioned in the introduction the original language was Hebrew. This language was given to the first man Adam and was eventually passed down through Adam's chosen lineage starting with Seth. According to the Book of Jubilees, the language of Hebrew is the language used in the heavens and was considered the language of creation.

Jubilees 12:24-27 And I shall be a God to thee and thy son, and to thy son's son, and to all thy seed: fear not, from henceforth and unto all generations of the earth I am thy God."

25 And the Lord God said: "Open his mouth and his ears, that he may hear and speak with his mouth, with the language which hath been revealed"; for it had ceased from the mouths of all the children of men from the day of the overthrow (of Babel).

26 And I opened his mouth, and his ears and his lips, and I began to speak with him in Hebrew in the tongue of the creation.

27 And he took the books of his fathers, and these were written in Hebrew and he transcribed them, and he began from henceforth to study them, and I made known to him that which he could not (understand), and he studied them during the six rainy months.

At one point in time, all nations of the earth spoke one language being Hebrew.

Genesis 11:1 And the whole earth was of one language, and of one speech.

The tongues were originally split into 70 different languages. This is document in both the Book of Jasher and the Testament of Naphtali, which can be read from the Pseudepigrapha.

The Most High God True Name

Moses asks the Most High God, what shall he say to the children of Israel when he goes to them and say "The God of your fathers hath sent me unto you" and the Most High said "I AM THAT I AM: and he said, Thus shalt thou say unto the children of Israel, I AM hath sent me unto you." The Father true name is AHAYAH ASHER AHAYAH in Hebrew.

Exodus 3:13-15 And Moses said unto God, Behold, when I come unto the children of Israel, and shall say unto them, The God of your fathers hath sent me unto you; and they shall say to me, What is his name? what shall I say unto them?

14 And God said unto Moses, I AM THAT I AM: and he said, Thus shalt thou say unto the children of Israel, I AM hath sent me unto you.

15 And God said moreover unto Moses, Thus shalt thou say unto the children of Israel, The LORD God of your fathers, the God of Abraham, the God of Isaac, and the God of Jacob, hath sent me unto you: this is my name for ever, and this is my memorial unto all generations.

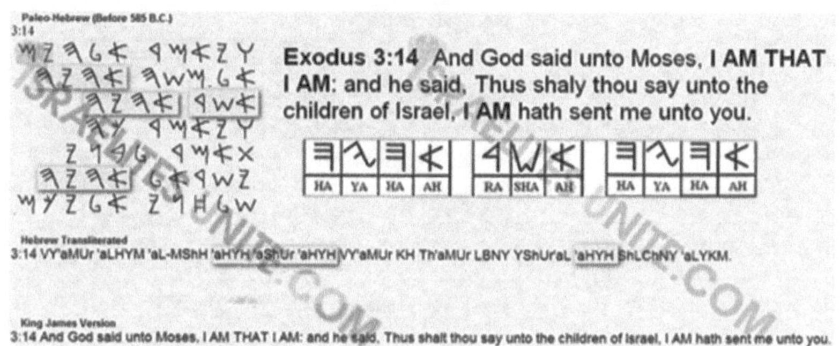

Ancient Hebrew (Above): this is the name our father gave Moses, AHAYAH ASHER AHAYAH.

In Exodus 3:15 he says "*this is my name for ever, and this is my memorial unto all generations*".

Exodus 3:15 And God said moreover unto Moses, Thus shalt thou say unto the children of Israel, The LORD God of your fathers, the God of Abraham, the God of Isaac, and the God of Jacob, hath sent me unto you: this is my name for ever, and this is my memorial unto all generations.

Christ True Name

In Acts 26:14 Paul heard Jesus (Yashaya) speak in the Hebrew tongue. The messiah was a Black Jew from the tribe of Judah as stated in Hebrews 7:14. The Messiah true name is YASHAYA in the Ancient Hebrew tongue.

Acts 26:14 And when we were all fallen to the earth, I heard a voice speaking unto me, and saying in the Hebrew tongue, Saul, Saul, why persecutest thou me? it is hard for thee to kick against the pricks.

PRINTING — THE ANCIENT HEBREW LANGUAGE

ENGLISH

THA	SHA	RA	QA	TAZA	PA	I	SA	NA	MA	LA	KA	YA	TA	CHAA	ZA	WA	HA	DA	GA	BA	AH

Pronunciation of the Hebrew letter, there is no letter J in the Hebrew Alphabet

PRINTING — THE ASSYRIAN HEBREW LANGUAGE

ת	ש	ר	ק	צ	פ	ע	ס	נ	מ	ל	כ	י	ט	ח	ז	ו	ה	ד	ג	ב	א
				ץ	ף			ן	ם		ך	USE THESE LETTERS IF LETTERS ABOVE FALL AT END OF WORD									

HANDWRITTEN

ת	ש	ר	ק	צ	פ	ע	ס	נ	מ	ל	כ	י	ט	ח	ז	ו	ה	ד	ג	ב	א
				ץ	ף			ן	ם		ך	USE THESE LETTERS IF LETTERS ABOVE FALL AT END OF WORD									

YA	SHA	YA

YASHAYA

Acts 4:12 Neither is there salvation in any other: for ther is none other name under heaven given among men, whereby we must be saved.

Precept:
Matthew 1:21 And she shall bring forth a son, and thou shalt call his name **YASHAYA**: for he shall save his people from their sins.

★6★

Holydays

Many celebrate pagan Holidays and not the true Holy Days that we are to keep and celebrate. The Most High God gave us these special days to observe from generation to generation, forever. The true Holy Days are in Leviticus Chapter 23 of the bible. The Bible tells us in Isaiah 14:12-14 that satan wants to be like The Most High God. The Most High God gives us Holydays to follow, and satan gives us pagan holidays to serve and worship him.

Ecclesiasticus 43:6-8 From the moon is the sign of feasts, a light that decreaseth in her perfection.

6 He made the moon also to serve in her season for a declaration of times, and a sign of the world.

7 From the moon is the sign of feasts, a light that decreaseth in her perfection.

8 The month is called after her name, increasing wonderfully in her changing, being an instrument

of the armies above, shining in the firmament of heaven; - *Authorized KJV Apocrypha*

Purim

This Feast of Purim commemorated the deliverance of the Jews from Haman while they were in captivity under Persian rule. Haman (Edomite so-called white man) was promoted in rank under King Ahasuerus. During the Kingdom of Persia and Media captivity in the reign of King Ahasuerus, Haman the son of Hammedatha, the Agagite, the enemy of all the Jews from the seed of Amalek (Est.3). Due to Haman's hatred towards Mordecia, he devised a plan against the Jews to destroy them, and had cast Purim, that is, the lot, to consume them, and to destroy them. Queen Esther (niece of Mordecai) made petition to king Ahasuerus to help deliver her people from the hands of Haman (Est. 7th). This Holy Day is celebrated by feasting and reading through the scriptures to get the history of the events that lead to the Jews being saved from their enemies by the Most High God and Mordecia and Esther. It is also a time to send gifts to each other read Ester 9:19.

Ester 9:13-32 Then said Esther, If it please the king, let it be granted to the Jews which are in Shushan to do to morrow also according unto this day's decree, and let Haman's ten sons be hanged upon the gallows.

14 And the king commanded it so to be done: and the decree was given at Shushan; and they hanged Haman's ten sons.

15 For the Jews that were in Shushan gathered themselves together on the fourteenth day also of the month Adar, and slew three hundred men at Shushan; but on the prey they laid not their hand.

16 But the other Jews that were in the king's provinces gathered themselves together, and stood

for their lives, and had rest from their enemies, and slew of their foes seventy and five thousand, but they laid not their hands on the prey,

17 On the thirteenth day of the month Adar; and on the fourteenth day of the same rested they, and made it a day of feasting and gladness.

18 But the Jews that were at Shushan assembled together on the thirteenth day thereof, and on the fourteenth thereof; and on the fifteenth day of the same they rested, and made it a day of feasting and gladness.

19 Therefore the Jews of the villages, that dwelt in the unwalled towns, made the fourteenth day of the month Adar a day of gladness and feasting, and a good day, and of sending portions one to another.

20 And Mordecai wrote these things, and sent letters unto all the Jews that were in all the provinces of the king Ahasuerus, both nigh and far,

21 To stablish this among them, that they should keep the fourteenth day of the month Adar, and the fifteenth day of the same, yearly,

22 As the days wherein the Jews rested from their enemies, and the month which was turned unto them from sorrow to joy, and from mourning into a good day: that they should make them days of feasting and joy, and of sending portions one to another, and gifts to the poor.

23 And the Jews undertook to do as they had begun, and as Mordecai had written unto them;

24 Because Haman the son of Hammedatha, the Agagite, the enemy of all the Jews, had devised against the Jews to destroy them, and had cast Pur, that is, the lot, to consume them, and to destroy them;

25 But when Esther came before the king, he commanded by letters that his wicked device, which he devised against the Jews, should return upon his own head, and that he and his sons should be hanged on the gallows.

26 Wherefore they called these days Purim after the name of Pur. Therefore for all the words of this letter, and of that which they had seen concerning this matter, and which had come unto them,

27 The Jews ordained, and took upon them, and upon their seed, and upon all such as joined themselves unto them, so as it should not fail, that they would keep these two days according to their writing, and according to their appointed time every year;

28 And that these days should be remembered and kept throughout every generation, every family, every province, and every city; and that these days of Purim should not fail from among the Jews, nor the memorial of them perish from their seed.

29 Then Esther the queen, the daughter of Abihail, and Mordecai the Jew, wrote with all authority, to confirm this second letter of Purim.

30 And he sent the letters unto all the Jews, to the hundred twenty and seven provinces of the kingdom of Ahasuerus, with words of peace and truth,

31 To confirm these days of Purim in their times appointed, according as Mordecai the Jew and Esther the queen had enjoined them, and as they had decreed for themselves and for their seed, the matters of the fastings and their cry.

32 And the decree of Esther confirmed these matters of Purim; and it was written in the book.

Feast of Unleavened Bread

(Passover)

The Passover is a Holy Day Feast in which we remember how the Most High God saved our forefathers from the hard bondage (400 years) in Egypt under Pharaoh by sending great wonders and plagues, and the last one was an Angel of death or death Angel. Those who had the blood of the lamb of Israel upon their door posts would be saved from that plague, but those that did not all the first born of the Egyptians and their cattle were slain by the angel of death. We are to celebrate the Passover by making a Holy Convocation and eating lamb made with fire, bitter herbs and unleavened bread. This should be done as closely as possible to how our fathers did it in Exodus the 12th chapter. We don't deal with the sacrificial part of the law anymore because Christ fulfilled this by dying for our sins on the cross. The feast of Unleavened Bread should also be celebrated by removing leaven (yeast) from your homes so we don't consume anything with leaven for seven days. For seven days we are to feast and celebrate but the 1st and 7th day shall be a Holy Convocation (gathering) as the scripture says. Please read more about the Feast of Unleavened Bread (Passover) in these scriptures: Leviticus 23:4-8,Exodus 12:1-27, Matthew 26:1-2, Numbers 9:1-7, Numbers 28:16-25, and also Deuteronomy 16:1-8.

Exodus 12:1-28 And the LORD spake unto Moses and Aaron in the land of Egypt, saying,

2 This month shall be unto you the beginning of months: it shall be the first month of the year to you.

3 Speak ye unto all the congregation of Israel, saying, In the tenth day of this month they shall take to them every man a lamb, according to the house of their fathers, a lamb for an house:

4 And if the household be too little for the lamb, let him and his neighbour next unto his house take it according to the number of the souls; every man according to his eating shall make your count for the lamb.

5 Your lamb shall be without blemish, a male of the first year: ye shall take it out from the sheep, or from the goats:

6 And ye shall keep it up until the fourteenth day of the same month: and the whole assembly of the congregation of Israel shall kill it in the evening.

7 And they shall take of the blood, and strike it on the two side posts and on the upper door post of the houses, wherein they shall eat it.

8 And they shall eat the flesh in that night, roast with fire, and unleavened bread; and with bitter herbs they shall eat it.

9 Eat not of it raw, nor sodden at all with water, but roast with fire; his head with his legs, and with the purtenance thereof.

10 And ye shall let nothing of it remain until the morning; and that which remaineth of it until the morning ye shall burn with fire.

11 And thus shall ye eat it; with your loins girded, your shoes on your feet, and your staff in your hand; and ye shall eat it in haste: it is the LORD'S passover.

12 For I will pass through the land of Egypt this night, and will smite all the firstborn in the land of Egypt, both man and beast; and against all the gods of Egypt I will execute judgment: I am the LORD.

13 And the blood shall be to you for a token upon the houses where ye are: and when I see the blood, I will pass over you, and the plague shall not be upon you to destroy you, when I smite the land of Egypt.

14 <u>And this day shall be unto you for a memorial; and ye shall keep it a feast to the LORD throughout your generations; ye shall keep it a feast by an ordinance for ever.</u>

15 Seven days shall ye eat unleavened bread; even the first day ye shall put away leaven out of your houses: for whosoever eateth leavened bread from the first day until the seventh day, that soul shall be cut off from Israel.

16 And in the first day there shall be an holy convocation, and in the seventh day there shall be an holy convocation to you; no manner of work shall be done in them, save that which every man must eat, tha only may be done of you.

17 And ye shall observe the feast of unleavened bread; for in this selfsame day have I brought your armies out of the land of Egypt: therefore shall ye observe this day in your generations by an ordinance for ever.

18 In the first month, on the fourteenth day of the month at even, ye shall eat unleavened bread, until the one and twentieth day of the month at even.

19 Seven days shall there be no leaven found in your houses: for whosoever eateth that which is leavened, even that soul shall be cut off from the congregation of Israel, whether he be a stranger, or born in the land.

20 Ye shall eat nothing leavened; in all your habitations shall ye eat unleavened bread.

21 Then Moses called for all the elders of Israel, and said unto them, Draw out and take you a lamb according to your families, and kill the passover.

22 And ye shall take a bunch of hyssop, and dip it in the blood that is in the bason, and strike the lintel and the two side posts with the blood that is in the bason; and none of you shall go out at the door of his house until the morning.

23 For the LORD will pass through to smite the Egyptians; and when he seeth the blood upon the lintel, and on the two side posts, the LORD will pass over the door, and will not suffer the destroyer to come in unto your houses to smite you.

24 And ye shall observe this thing for an ordinance to thee and to thy sons for ever.

25 And it shall come to pass, when ye be come to the land which the LORD will give you, according as he hath promised, that ye shall keep this service.

26 And it shall come to pass, when your children shall say unto you, What mean ye by this service?

27 That ye shall say, It is the sacrifice of the LORD'S passover, who passed over the houses of the children of Israel in Egypt, when he smote the Egyptians, and delivered our houses. And the people bowed the head and worshipped.

28 And the children of Israel went away, and did as the LORD had commanded Moses and Aaron, so did they.

Feast of the First Fruits

The Feast of the First Fruits is celebrated after the day of the Passover, seven Sabbaths later is the feast of Pentecost also called the Feast of Weeks. The children of Israel would offer a free will offering unto the Most High God according to how much he had blessed their harvest with increase. This was celebrated by offering the first fruits of all that was produced and bringing them to the Levites for a free will offering to the Most High. This was a time when all Israel would gather in Jerusalem to celebrate the Holy Convocation. In today's world we would celebrate this Holy Day by feasting and remembering the feast of First Fruits (Pentecost) in which the Disciples received the gift of the Holy Spirit. Please read more about the Feast of the First Fruits in these scriptures: Deuteronomy 16:9-12, Acts 2:1-11, and Leviticus 23:9-22.

Exodus 23:16 And the feast of harvest, the firstfruits of thy labours, which thou hast sown in the field: and the feast of ingathering, *which is* in the end of the year, when thou hast gathered in thy labours out of the field.

Exodus 34:22 And thou shalt observe the feast of weeks, of the firstfruits of wheat harvest, and the feast of ingathering at the year's end.

Memorial of Blowing Trumpets

The Memorial of Blowing the Trumpets is when the children of Israel would blow the trumpets at the beginnings of Months and to go to war they would sound or blow the trumpet and the Most High God would remember them before they go to war and would save them from their enemies. We are to celebrate this Holy Day by having a Holy Convocation and to feast unto the Most High God. Please read more about the Memorial of Blowing Trumpets in these scriptures: Numbers 29:1-6, Numbers 10:9-10, Maccabees 2:5-8. Deuteronomy 16:13-16.

> **Leviticus 23:23-25 And the LORD spake unto Moses, saying,**
>
> **24 Speak unto the children of Israel, saying, In the seventh month, in the first day of the month, shall ye have a sabbath, amemorial ofblowing oftrumpets, an holy convocation.**
>
> **25 Ye shall do no servile work therein: but ye shall offer an offering made by fire unto the LORD.**

Day of Atonement

The Day of Atonement is a day that the Most High requires the Israelites to fast or afflict their souls, this is done once a year to make an atonement for the sins they had committed the whole year. The Day of Atonement is observed on the Seventh month 10th day by having a Sabbath and every soul must be afflicted (Fast). It is a Holy Convocation throughout your generations. We celebrate this Holy Day by having a Holy Convocation in which we do no servile work and we are to afflict our souls with fasting and prayer. Please read more about the Day of Atonement in these scriptures: Numbers 29:7-11, Isaiah Chapter 58, and Matthew 6:16-18.

Leviticus 23:26-32 And the LORD spake unto Moses, saying,

27 Also on the tenth day of this seventh month there shall be a day of atonement: it shall be an holy convocation unto you; and ye shall afflict your souls, and offer an offering made by fire unto the LORD.

28 And ye shall do no work in that same day: for it is a day of atonement, to make an atonement for you before the LORD your God.

29 For whatsoever soul it be that shall not be afflicted in that same day, he shall be cut off from among his people.

30 And whatsoever soul it be that doeth any work in that same day, the same soul will I destroy from among his people.

31 Ye shall do no manner of work: it shall be a statute for ever throughout your generations in all your dwellings.

32 It shall be unto you a sabbath of rest, and ye shall afflict your souls: in the ninth day of of the month at even, from even unto even, shall ye celebrate your sabbath.

Feast of Tabernacles

The Feast of Tabernacles is a feast that the Most High God requires Israel to have a celebration to commemorate their wandering in the wilderness for forty years. The First day is a Sabbath and the last day is a Sabbath. The Most High required Israel to dwell in booths made out of boughs of trees and branches of palm trees, to commemorate our dwelling in booths in the wilderness. The first and the eight day are to be a Holy Convocations. Please read more about the Feast of Tabernacles in these scriptures: Deuteronomy 16:13-16, and 2 Maccabees 2:5-8.

Leviticus 23:33-44 And the LORD spake unto Moses, saying,

34 Speak unto the children of Israel, saying, The fifteenth day of this seventh month shall be the feast of tabernacles for seven days unto the LORD.

35 On the first day shall be an holy convocation: ye shall do no servile work therein.

36 Seven days ye shall offer an offering made by fire unto the LORD: on the eighth day shall be an holy convocation unto you; and ye shall offer an offering made by fire unto the LORD: it is a solemn assembly; and ye shall do no servile work therein.

37 These are the feasts of the LORD, which ye shall proclaim to be holy convocations, to offer an offering made by fire unto the LORD, a burnt offering, and a meat offering, a sacrifice, and drink offerings, everything upon his day:

38 Beside the sabbaths of the LORD, and beside your gifts, and beside all your vows, and beside all your freewill offerings, which ye give unto the LORD.

39 Also in the fifteenth day of the seventh month, when ye have gathered in the fruit of the land, ye shall keep a feast unto the LORD seven days: on the first day shall be a sabbath, and on the eighth day shall be a sabbath.

40 And ye shall take you on the first day the boughs of goodly trees, branches of palm trees, and the boughs of thick trees, and willows of the brook; and ye shall rejoice before the LORD your God seven days.

41 And ye shall keep it a feast unto the LORD seven days in the year. It shall be a statute for ever in your generations: ye shall celebrate it in the seventh month.

42 Ye shall dwell in booths seven days; all that are Israelites born shall dwell in booths:

43 That your generations may know that I made the children of Israel to dwell in booths, when I brought them out of the land of Egypt: I am the LORD your God.

44 And Moses declared unto the children of Israel the feasts of the LORD.

Feast of Dedication (Hanukkah)

The Feast of Dedication is a Holy Day in remembrance of that and how Jonathan Maccabee lead our people into fighting against this tyranny of the Greeks and us rededicating the temple to the Most High once we gained control over our land again. During the time of the Maccabees after Antiochus and the Greeks had defiled the temple of the Most High God and made it law that the children of Israel could no longer follow the commandments of the Most High. They began to profane the temple by Greeks sacrificing swine and other abominations in the temple. We are to celebrate this feast by having a Holy Convocation to the Most High God. Please read more about Hanukkah / Feast of Dedication (Feast of Lights) in these scriptures: 1 Maccabees 4:52-59, 2 Maccabees Chapter 4th.

Hanukkah - A dedication.

John 10:22 And it was at Jerusalem the <u>feast of the dedication</u>, and it was winter

★7★

Days and Months Meaning

Month is named after "Munt", which originally was the local deity of Hermonthis. Hermonthis, Ancient City, N Egypt, 8 mi (13 km) S of Thebes. It was founded in prehistoric times and was prominent during the period of Roman supremacy. Originally the shrine of Month, later the war-god of the Egyptian king; represented as falcon-headed. America gets all of their Symbols and Signs from the Ancient Babylonians and the Egyptians. Everything is based and or leading back to a Pagan God.

Psalm 96:4-5 For the LORD is great, and greatly to be praised: he is to be feared above all gods.

5 For all the gods of the nations are idols: but the LORD made the heavens.

Januray, Named after Janus, Roman god of doors and gates. Janus, in Roman religion, god of beginnings. He was one of the principal Roman gods, the custodian of the universe. The first hour of the day, the first day of the month, the first month of the year (which bears his name) were sacred to him. His chief function was as guardian deity of gates and doors. The gates of his temple in the Roman Forum were closed in time of peace and opened in time of war. Janus was usually represented with two bearded heads placed back to back so that he might look in two directions at the same time. His principal festival was celebrated on the first day of the year.

February, Named after Februa, Roman period of purification. Februa, also Februatio was the Roman festival of purification, also commonly referred to as Lupercalia (see for more complete information on the holiday). The festival, which is basically one of Spring washing or cleaning (associated also with the raininess of this time of year) is old, and possibly of Sabine origin. According to Ovid, Februare as a Latin word which refers to means of purification (particularly with washing or water) derives from an earlier Etruscan word referring to purging The Roman month Februarius ("of Februa," whence the English February) is named for the Februa/Februatio festival, which occurred on the 15th day of the Roman month. A later Roman god Februus personified both the month and also purification, and is named for them. Thus, the month is named for the festival and not for the god.

March, Named after Mars, Roman god of war. Mars, in Roman religion and mythology, god of war. In early Roman times he was a god of agriculture, but in later religion (when he was identified with the Greek Ares) he was primarily associated with war. Mars was the father of Romulus, the founder of the Roman nation, and, next to Jupiter, he enjoyed the highest position in Roman religion. The Salii, his priests, honored him by dancing in full armor in the Campus Martius, the site of his altar. Chariot races and the sacrifice of animals were primary features of the festivals held in his honor in March (named for him) and October. Mars was represented as an armed warrior. His attributes include the spear and shield, and the wolf and woodpecker were sacred to him. He was frequently associated with Bellona, the Roman goddess of war.

April, from the Latin apeire, 'to open'. Apéritif is a French word, which, like its Italian counterpart, aperitivo, comes from the Latin aperire, meaning "to open." because spring generally begins, and the buds open in this month.

May, Named after Maia, Roman goddess of spring and growth. Maia, 1 In Greek mythology, oldest of the Pleiades. She was the mother of Hermes by Zeus. 2 In Roman mythology, goddess of fertility; also called Maiesta. She was often identified with Bona Dea. The month of May was probably named for her.

June, Named after Juno, Roman goddess of marriage. The chief goddess and female counterpart of Jupiter. She was identified with the Greek goddess Hera. With Jupiter and Minerva she was a member of the Capitoline triad of deities traditionally introduced into Rome by the Etruscans. She was connected with all aspects of the lives of women, particularly marriage. Individualized, she became a female guardian spirit; as every man had his genius, so every woman had her juno. Her temple in Rome eventually housed the Roman mint, and she was invoked as the savior of the state. Her sacred bird was the peacock.

July, Named after Julias Caesar. From Latin Iulius "fifth month of the Roman calendar" (which began its year in March),renamed after his death and deification in honor of Gaius Julius Caesar, whowas born in this month, which formerly in republican Rome was namedQuintilis "fifth." Accented on first syllable in English until 18 century.

August, Named after Augustus, first emperor of Rome. Augustus, 63 B.C. - A.D. 14, first Roman emperor, a grandson of the sister of Julius Caesar. Named at first Caius Octavius, he became on adoption by the Julian gens (44 B.C.) Caius Julius Caesar Octavianus (Octavian); Augustus was a title of honor granted (27 B.C.) by the senate.

September, from the Latin septem, 'seven'. September is the magical seventh month in the original ten-month Roman calendar. It was the time of the Ludi Romani, the great games in honour of Jove (Jupiter) which ran from the 5-19 of the month. The games were spectacular affairs beginning with parades to honour the gods and culminating with chariot races at the Circus Maximus.

October, from the Latin octo, 'eight'. October is the tenth month of the year in the Gregorian Calendar and one of seven Gregorian months with a length of 31 days. The eighth month in the old Roman calendar, October retained its name (from the Greek "octo" meaning "eight") when January and February were added. October was a month of many festivals to honour Jupiter and Juno. As Jupiter was a wine god, much wine was consumed in his honour and celebrations often got out of hand. Apart from wine, feasts and games were also held in the god's honour and these were open to everyone. Sacrifices were offered on the field of Mars.

November, from the Latin novem, 'nine'. September is the ninth month of the year in the Gregorian Calendar and one of four Gregorian months with 30 days. d In Latin, septem means "seven" and septimus means "seventh"; September was in fact the seventh month of the Roman calendar until 153 BC, when there was a calendar reform from the month of the Ides of March to the Kalends, or January 1. November was considered a lucky month as it was virtually free of any religious obligation. It was traditionally the beginning of the Roman winter and a time for many festivals of feasting, games and wine drinking.

December, from the Latin decem, 'ten'. December is the twelfth and last month of the year in the Gregorian Calendar and one of seven Gregorian months with the length of 31 days. In Latin, decem means "ten". December was also the tenth month in the Roman calendar until a monthless winter period was divided between January and February. December began with the festival of Neptune, the god of sea and water, or Poseidon to the Greeks. The end of December signified the beginning of the solar year. During December the Romans observed the 'Halycon Days', seven days of peace and calm prior to the Winter Solstice and another seven days after it.

Meaning of the Days of Weeks

The English names of all of the days of the week come from Anglo-Saxon polytheism.

Sunday - Named after the Sun. Sunday, Latin dies solis ("day of the sun"), which is a translation of of Greek heméra helíou. The 1st day of the week.

Monday - Named after the Moon. Monday, Latin lunae dies ("day of the moon"). The 2nd day of the week.

Tuesday - Named after Tiu, the Norse god of war. Tuesday ("Day of Mars,") from the Roman god of war, who was identified with Gmc. The 3rd day of the week.

Wednesday - Named after Woden, the Anglo-Saxon chief of the gods. The name Wednesday comes from the Middle English Wednes dei, which is from Old English language Wēdnes dæg, meaning the day of the English god Woden (Wodan) who was a god of the Anglo-Saxons in England until about the 7th century. Wēdnes dæg is like the Old Norse Oðinsdagr ("Odin's day"), which is an early translation of the Latin dies Mercurii ("Mercury's day"), and reflects the widespread association of Woden with Mercury going back to Tacitus. In Romance languages it is derived from the name of the Roman god Mercury. The 4th day of the week;

Thursday - Named after Thor, Norse god of thunder. Thursday comes from the Old English Thursdæg, literally: Thor's day. The name of the Germanic god Thor comes from the Old Norse word for thunder. ("Jupiter Day"). The 5th day of the week.

Friday - Named after Freyja, a Norse goddess of love. The meaning of Frige the Anglo-Saxon form of Frigg, a West Germanic translation of Latin dies Veneris, "day (of the planet) Venus." The 6th day of the week. ("Venus Day")

Saturday - Named after Saturn, Roman god of harvests and time. The planet (Saturn), which controlled the first hour of that day according to Vettius Valens. The planet was named for the Roman god of agriculture Saturn. It has been called dies Saturni ("Saturn's Day"), through which from it entered into Old English as Sæternesdæg and gradually evolved into the word "Saturday". The 7th day of the week.

★ 8 ★

Pagan Holidays

All Holidays are pagan as well as your Birthday celebration. People across the world celebrate these evil Holidays. Do you know where the word Holiday comes from? Holiday comes from the word Holy-day. There is nothing holy about these Holidays in America. The true Holy days are in Leviticus 23rd chapter of the bible as I have shown in chapter 3 of this book.

Christmas

Christmas is the so called celebration of Christ when he was born. In Roman it was a celebration of his death, not of his birth. In fact the Bible tells us that the Messiah was born in the springtime, not the winter. In fact the date of Christmas (Dec 25) is related to the winter solstice in the Northern hemisphere. The day of December 25th is a pagan satanic holiday Nimrod the ancient Babylonian ruler and his son Tammuz is worshipped on that day, as the sun god. The Christmas tree is a pagan ritual. Nimrod the god of the Babylonians and Assyrians and his son Tammuz were symbolized in the form of palm trees after their death. Christmas is nothing but idol worship. Did you know if you bring a Christmas tree in your house it's an abomination to the Most High God?, stated in Jeremiah 10:1-5 and Deuteronomy 7:25-26.

> **Jeremiah 10:1-5 Hear ye the word which the LORD speaketh unto you, O house of Israel:**
>
> **2 Thus saith the LORD, Learn not the way of the heathen, and be not dismayed at the signs of heaven; for the heathen are dismayed at them.**
>
> **3 For the customs of people are vain: for one cutteth a tree out of a forest, the work of the hands of the workman, with the ax.**
>
> **4 They deck it with silver and with gold; they fasten it with nails and with hammers, that it move not.**
>
> **5 They are upright as the palm tree, but speak not: thy must needs be borne, because they cannot go. Be not afraid of them; for they cannot do evil, neither also is it in them to do good.**

Vain- Without real significance, value, or importance; baseless or worthless.

Borne- To hold or remain firm under.

Verse three says "For the customs of people are vain". This verse means, what people are doing have no real significance, it's pointless. Also in verse 5 it says "thy must needs be borne". This is clearly referring to a Christmas tree stand.

Jeremiah 10:1 Hear ye the word which the Most High speaketh unto you, O house of Isarel
SANTA
IS SATAN SPELLED INSIDE OUT
Palm Tree
Borne
Jeremiah 10:3 For the customs of people are vain: for one cutteth a tree out of the forest, the work of the hands of the workman, with the axe.
Jeremiah 10:4 They deck it with silver and gold; they fasten it with nails and with hammers, that it move not.
Jeremiah 10:5 They are upright as the palm tree; but speak not: they must needs be borne, because they cannot go. be not afraid of them; for they cannot do evil, neither also is it in them to do good.
WWW.ISRAELITESUNITE.COM

This verse is letting us know that the Most High God hates such an act when one brings a Christmas tree in their House. In verse 26 it says "Neither shalt thou bring an abomination into thine house, lest thou be cursed thing like it:" This statement is very clear, simply do not bring these false images and deities into your house, unless you want to be cursed like them.

> **Deuteronomy 7:25-26 The graven images of their gods shall ye burn with fire: thou shalt not desire the silver or gold that is on them, nor take it unto thee, lest thou be snared therein: for it is an abomination to the LORD thy God.**
>
> **26 Neither shalt thou bring an abomination into thine house, lest thou be cursed thing like it: but thou shalt utterly detest it, and thou shalt utterly abhor it; for it is a cursed thing.**

Abomination - feeling of disgust, hatred, loathing.

Easter

Easter is a so called annual Christian festival in commemoration of the resurrection of Jesus Christ, observed on the first Sunday. This is False and a lie. Easter in fact comes from the words Eastre,

Eastre, Ashtoreth, Astarte, or Ishtar. Nimrod and his wife Semiramis. They made many satanic and wicked religious practices, like, Idol worship, satan worship, human sacrifice, astrology, sun, moon, and star worship, and witchcraft. In truth the Easter holiday is really a celebration of the resurrection of Semiramis son Tammuz. The Re-incarnation of Nimrod in the springtime. One must ask the question, where did Easter Egg come from? The Egg is one of the many false idols of the ancient Babylonians. The egg for them symbolized fertility and Semiramis, the false pagan goddess of fertility spread this pagan custom to many nations and peoples. Where did the Easter rabbit come from? The rabbit is another symbol that represents fertility. Remember rabbits don't lay eggs.

> **1 Samuel 7:3 And Samuel spake unto all the house of Israel, saying, If ye do return unto the LORD with all your hearts, *then*put away the strange gods and <u>Ashtaroth</u> from among you, and prepare your hearts unto the LORD, and serve him only: and he will deliver you out of the hand of the Philistines.**

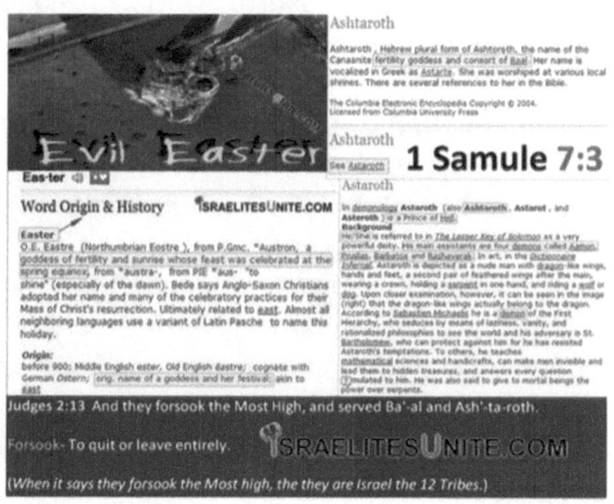

Thanksgiving

The whole concept of thanksgiving derived from the English Colonialist on July 30, 1621. Governor William Bradford, issued a proclamation calling for a Thanksgiving celebration feast, to commemorate the gathering of the first harvest, which lasted three days. The Most High God condemns anyone who celebrates Thanksgiving, or goes to a Thanksgiving Day parade, or eats a Thanksgiving dinner in the name of the Most High God. Thanksgiving was a prelude to the massacre and slaughter of the North American Indians (Tribe of Gad) Infants were torn from their mother's breast and hacked to pieces. The victory seemed a sweet sacrifice and they gave praise to their ('their god'). The 'pilgrims' didn't want religious freedom they wanted wealth. The 'pilgrims' were murderers, rapists, thieves, child molesters, homosexuals, whores, prostitutes, drunks, and insane lowlifes, who brought syphilis, gonorrhea, tuberculosis, small pox, etc. They infected the North American Indians with these diseases and killed millions of them. These 'pilgrims' who are white Europeans. In conclusion to all of this the pilgrims (so-called white man) came to steal their land, kill and to destroy the North American Indians and they celebrate it with Thanksgiving.

> **John 10:10 The <u>thief cometh not but for to steal, and to kill, and to destroy</u>: I am come that they might have life, and that they might have it more abundantly.**

You must also remember that in the autumn of 1621 when Plymouth governor William Bradford invited neighboring Indians to join the Pilgrims for a three-day festival of recreation and feasting and that's when they the 'pilgrims' had instead murdered, tortured, butured, and enslaved them. The "pilgrims" used words like "we come in peace" and "we love you" to fool the Indians. It was all a lie. The "pilgrims" (Esau) stole their and. Look what John 10:10 says again, that's what the pilgrims did to the North American Indians.

Micah 2:1-2 Woe to them that devise iniquity, and work evil upon their beds! when the morning is light, they practise it, because it is in the power of their hand.

2 And they covet fields, and take them by violence; and houses, and take them away: so they oppress a man and his house, even a man and his heritage.

Devise - To contrive, plan, or elaborate; invent from existing principles or ideas.

Iniquity - A grossly immoral act; a sin.

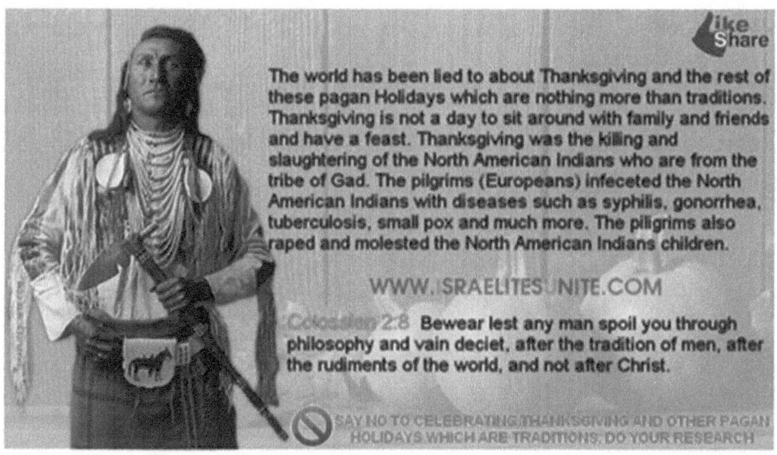

Halloween

The word Halloween Originally comes from medieval England's All Hallows' Eve (Old Eng.*hallow*="saint"), the eve of All Saints' Day. Its pagan origins can be traced to the Celtic festival of Samhain. A night for witchcraft. The souls of the dead were supposed to revisit their homes on Samhain eve, and witches, goblins, black cats, and ghosts were said to roam about on that night. The night was also thought to be the most favorable time for divinations concerning marriage, luck, health, and death. These pagan observances influenced the Christian festival of All Hallows' Eve and that's when they started to celebrate this pagan holiday on the same day. This holiday was then introduced into the United States in the late 19th century.

Samhain - October 31, Halloween; a day of celebration for Wiccans and other pagans.

Witchcraft - The art or practices of a witch; sorcery; magic.

Divinations - the practice of attempting to foretell future events or discover hidden knowledge by occult or supernatural means.

This holiday is still associated with evil spirits and the supernatural. It is also still celebrated by children in costume who gather candy by ringing doorbells and calling out **'trick or treat**," "**trick**" referring to the pranks and vandalism from this pagan holiday.

Prank- A trick of an amusing, playful, or sometimes malicious nature.

Vandalism- Deliberately mischievous or malicious destruction or damage of property.

New Year's

New Year's Day in modern America was not always on January 1st. New Year's is the oldest of all holidays; it was first observed about 4,000 years ago by the Ancient Babylon. Babylonian New Year began with the first New Moon around 2,000 BC on the first day of spring. The beginning of spring is a logical time to start a new year, because it is the season of rebirth, of plating new crops, and them blooming. January 1st is nothing more than a deception and a lie including this pagan holiday New Year's. Also the Babylonians New Year lasted for 11 days. The Romans continued to observe the New Year in late March. The Roman calendar was changed so much that it got of order with the sun. In 46 BC Julius Caesar established the Julian calendar. After that he celebrated the first on January 1st by ordering the violent routing of revolutionary Jewish forces in the Galilee. In later years the Roman pagans observed the New Year by engaging in drunken orgies.

So why did Caesar name the first month January? He did these to pay homage to the Roman God of doors and gates and the same god that had two faces. Janus was a dual headed god. The dual heads, one looking forward and one looking behind represents actual and metaphorical threshold in time and space.

Saturnalia - 1. The ancient Roman seven-day festival of Saturn, which began on December 17.

2. Celebration marked by unrestrained revelry and often licentiousness; an orgy.

Actual statue of the Roman God (Janus)

The early Babylonians most popular resolution was to return borrowed farm equipment. This has to do with the spring connection I mentioned early. The tradition of using a baby to signify the New Year had begun in Greece. The early Christians denounced the practice as pagan. The church finally allowed the members to celebrate the New Year with a baby. The Year before the council of Nicaea convened, Sylvester convinced Constantine to prohibit Jews from living in Jerusalem. At the council of nicaea, Sylvester arranged for the passage of a host of viciously Anti-Semitic legislation. All Catholic "Saints" are awarded a day o which Christians celebrate and pay tribute to that saints memory. December 31 is Saint Sylvester day. In conclusion we shouldn't be celebrating New Years because it is an abomination unto Yahweh our Heavenly Father.

Valentines

Valentine come from the Latin (Valentinus), which derives from the word Valens-Latin, meaning: strong, powerful, *healthy / able, worthwhile,* and that famous man is Lupercus. The Greeks called Lupercus by the name of pan, god of light. The month of February was sacred to Juno Februata, the Goddess of the febris "*fever*" *of love* in ancient Pagan Rome. She was also the goddess of women and of marriage. February 14 was her festival day. Remember the evening of February 14, At that time, a box was provided from which single men could draw a billet- *a small piece of paper on which a woman's name was written on it,* where put into a container. The Teen -aged boys would then pull out a billet at random. They would then become couples from that point on. They then would remain sexual partnrs until the rest of the festival. In 494 AD Pope Gelasius renamed a cleaned-up festival the "*Feast of the Purification of the Virgin Mary.*" Feburay 14 was then changed to Feburary 2. It is now called the *Presentation of the Lord.*

Cupid is nothing but another word for Nimrod. It comes from the Latin word Cupido "desire, love," from cupere "to desire". Cupid was Venus, a Roman goddess of beauty and love. Also known as Eros in Ancient Greece. Cupid was a child-like archor.

There is allot of money to be made of this pagan holiday. Valentine's Day was dropped from the Catholic calendar 1969.

Actual Statue of Romulus & Remus getting fed by a She-Wolf

St. Valentine's Day can be traced back to *Lupercalia*, the Roman "***festival of sexual license.***" although it might have been associated with protection from wolves (*lupus* in Latin). The dog was probably a substitute for a wolf. The celebration was held in the Lupercal cave on the Palatine Hill in Rome. Here, it was believed, Romulus and Remus had been sheltered and fed by a she-wolf before they founded Rome. Two naked young priests, assisted by Vestal Virgins, would sacrifice a dog and a goat. The dog was probably a substitute for a wolf. The priests then clothed themselves with loincloths made from the skin of the goat. They ran about Rome, courging women with **februa-** *Latin for "means of purification"*. The Romans believed that this flogging would purify them, and assure their future fertility and easy childbirth.

★ 9 ★

Image of Christ

A Father afflicted with untimely mourning, that's Rodrigo Borgia, When he mad and image of his child, that's in reference to his son Cesare Borgia image put up to be Christ, which is how they honored him as a God though he was a dead man in Rome. They used this false image of Cesare Borgia as Christ, and they brought forth a false teaching and ceremonies and sacrifices and holidays all along with this image, to deceive the people. Christ was not a so called White man, but

> **Wisdom of Solomon 14:15 For a father afflicted with untimely mourning, when he hath made an image of his child soon taken away, now honoured him as a god, which was then a dead man, and delivered to those that were under him ceremonies and sacrifices.** – *Authorized KJV Apocrypha*

This is Cesare Borgia as Christ. The Image you see across the World.

Christ Was a Jew

The Samaria woman said unto the Messiah, "How is it that thou, being a Jew, askest drink of me, which am a woman of Samaria? For the Jews have no dealings with the Samaritans". This shows us that the Messiah was a Jew, because the women said "How is it that thou, being a Jew," She clearly knew that the Messiah was a Jew. Also the word Jew comes from the tribe of Judah. By us identifying what Nationality the Messiah was we can know identify his color. The tribe of Judah is the so called Negroes of America who are Black and from the seed of Abraham who also was a Jew or Hebrew Israelite.

> **John 4:9-10 Then saith the woman of Samaria unto him, How is it that thou, being a Jew, askest drink of me, which am a woman of Samaria? for the Jews have no dealings with the Samaritans.**
>
> **10 Jesus answered and said unto her, If thou knewest the gift of the Most High, and who it is that saith to thee, Give me to drink; thou wouldest have asked of him, and he would have given thee living water.**

Real Appearance of Christ

Let us examine the real image of Christ, instead of image that they put up as Christ, which is a so called white man. Let us examine Christ eyes and teeth according to scripture.

> **Genesis 49:12 His eyes shall be red with wine, and his teeth white with milk.**

We also read that Christ appearance was like unto fine brass. We know that fine brass is brown. See scripture below.

> **Ezekiel 40:3 And he brought me thither, and behold, there was a man, whose appearance of brass, with a line of flax in hand, and a measuring reed; and he stood in the gate.**

In Daniel 10 verse 5 and 6, Daniel said Christ arms and feet were the color of polished brass.

> **Daniel 10:5-6 Then I lifted up mine eyes, and looked, behold a certain man clothed in linen, whose loins were girded with fin gold of Uphaz:**
>
> **6 His body also was like the beryl, and his face as the apperance of lightning, and his eyes as lamps of fire, and his arms and feet like colour to polished brass, and the voice of his words like the voice of a multitude.**

The below verse describes Christ hair texture. The scripture tells us that his hair was like wool. Ask yourself this, what nationality of people has hair like wool? That nationality is the so called Negros.

> **Daniel 7:9 I beheld till the thrones were cast down, and the Ancient of days did sit, whose garment was white as snow, and the hair of his had like the**

pure wool: his throne was like the fiery flame, and his wheels as burning fire.

In Revelations chapter 1 we read that Christ feets was like unto fine brass. We know that fine brass is brownish dark black. This means that his feets were black. As pointed out in Revelation chapter 1 verse 14 and 15.

Revelations 1:14-15 His head and his hairs were white like wool, as white as snow; and his eyes were as a flame of fire;

15 And his feet like unto fine brass, as if they had burned in a furnace; and his voice as the sound of many waters.

We must understand that Christ (Messiah) was from the Tribe of Judah who is the so called African Americans, who are so called Black. This lets us know that Christ is a Black man who was a Jew from the tribe of Judah.

Hebrews 7:14 For it is evident that our Lord srpang out of juda: of which tribe Moses spake nothing concerning priesthood.

★ 10 ★

King James

King James was a King of Great Britain France and Ireland. He was a Black man and the King James Bible is named after King James I of England, who lived from June 19, 1566 to March 27, 1625. The Established Church was divided during this era. In 1603, King James called a conference in the Hampton Court in attempt to resolve issues. As a result, a new translation and compilation of approved books of the Bible was commissioned to resolve issues with translations then being used. For example, the Geneva Version contained controversial marginal notes that proclaimed the Pope as an anti-Christ. The leaders of the church desired a Bible for the people, with scriptural references only for word clarification or cross-references. Many may or may not know that He designed the British flag in 1603 by combining England's red cross of St. George with Scotland's white cross of St. Andrew.

King James approved 54 scholars to work on the translation, and 47 worked in six groups at three locations for seven years, comparing to previous English translations (such as the Geneva Bible) and texts in the original languages. The new translation was published in 1611 and called the Authorized Version, because it was authorized to be read in the churches. It later became known as the King James Version. The King

James translation had a significant influence on the English language and was widely accepted as the Standard English Bible. Because of the project being overseen by King James and the care and precise attention to detail during this seven-year translation, the King James Bible was considered one of the most accurate translations in existence.

Was King James A Homosexual?

No, Sir Anthony Weldon (1583–1648) who was an English 17th Century courtier and politician, and author of The Court and Character of King James I, wrote a paper calling James a homosexual. Obviously, James, being dead, was in no condition to defend himself. Weldon swore vengeance. It was not until 1650; twenty-five years after the death of King James that Weldon saw his chance. The report was largely ignored since there were still enough people alive who knew it wasn't true. It seems though, that Weldon's false account is being once again largely ignored by the majority of so called (Christians) with the exception of those with an ulterior motive, such as its author had. It might also be mentioned here that the Roman Catholic Church was so desperate to keep the true Bible out of the hands of the English people that it attempted to kill King James and all of Parliament in 1605. In 1605 a Roman Catholic by the name of Guy Fawkes, under the direction of a Jesuit priest by the name of Henry Garnet, was found in the basement of Parliament with thirty-six barrels of gunpowder which he was to use to blow up King James and the entire Parliament. After killing the king, they planned on imprisoning his children, re-establishing England as a state loyal to the Pope and kill all who resisted. Needless to say, the perfect English Bible would have been one of the plot's victims. Fawkes and Garnet and eight other conspirators were caught and hanged. It seems that those who work so hard to discredit the character of King James join an unholy lot. In conclusion we can see that King James wasn't a Homosexual and it was Sir Anthony Weldon who called him one in his Book, The Court and Character of King James I to seek vengeance on the great King James.

Conclusion

King James I of England, who authorized the translation of the now famous King James Bible, was considered by many to be one of the greatest, if not the greatest, monarchs that England has ever seen. King James I was a black man, and many of his surviving paintings falsely depict him as a so-called white man in clear contradiction to the famous description of the jolly King. Through his wisdom and determination he united the warring tribes of Scotland into a unified nation, and then joined England and Scotland to form the foundation for what is now known as the British Empire. At a time when only the churches of England possessed the Bible in English, King James' desire was that the common people should have the Bible in their native tongue. Thus, in 1603, King James called 54 of history's most learned men together to accomplish this great task. At a time when the leaders of the world wished to keep their subjects in spiritual ignorance, King James offered his subjects the greatest gift that he could give them. He offered them their own copy of the Word of the Most High in English. James, who was fluent in Latin, Greek, and French, and schooled in Italian and Spanish even wrote a tract entitled "Counterblast to Tobacco", which was written to help thwart the use of tobacco in England. Such a man was sure to have enemies.

★ 11 ★

The Letter J

The first English-language book to make a clear distinction between I and J was published in 1634 (Ref). Its use in the English alphabet followed, the letter J was the last of the 26 letters to be added to the English Alphabet. Its emerging distinctive use dates back to Middle High German, originally being a typographical flourish or swash character on the Roman i. The Italian: Gian Giorgio Trissino (1478-1550) was the first to explicitly distinguish I and J as representing separate sounds in 1524 with his "Trissino's epistle about the letters recently added in the Italian language.

The Messiah name isn't Jesus, that's a different god. We must be very carefully to who we are calling on if we are truly following the Messiah and his righteousness. The enemy is defaming Christ with a Pagan Name, by replacing his Hebrew name with a pagan Greek name that honors a pagan god. The name Jesus comes from Iesous which mean Hail Zeus. Zeus was a popular god in Graeco-Roman world. The Greek god Zeus who is a representation of The Sun god who is The Devil as known by ancient cultures. The Messiah name came from The Roman god Iesous. Also what we must understand is that even in the Authorized King James Bible it tells us that the Messiah spoke Hebrew:

Acts 26:14 And when we were all fallen to the earth, I heard a voice speaking unto me, and saying in the Hebrew tongue, Saul, Saul, why persecutest thou me? it is hard for thee to kick against the pricks.

In Acts 26:14 we read that Paul heard Jesus (Yashaya) speak in the Hebrew tongue. If the Messiah spoke Hebrew then his name must be Hebrew as well. The Messiah true name is YASHAYA in the Ancient Hebrew tongue.

hrift is tempted, S.Luke. He preacheth

ouercommeth the deuill : 14 Beginneth to preach : 16 The people of Nazareth admire his gratious words : 33 he cureth one possessed of a deuill, 38 Peters mother in law, 40 and diuers other sicke persons. 41 The deuils acknowledge Christ, and are reproued for it : 43 he preacheth through the cities.

Math. 4. AND *Iesus being full of
the holy Ghost, returned
from Iordane, and was
led by the spirit into the
wildernesse,
2 Being fourtie dayes tempted of
the deuil, and in those dayes he did eat
nothing : and when they were ended,
he afterward hungred.
3 And the deuil saide vnto him, If
thou be the Sonne of God, command
this stone that it be made bread.
4 And Iesus answered him, saying, It is written, that man shall not
liue by bread alone, but by euery word
of God.
5 And the deuil taking him vp into
an high mountaine, shewed vnto him
all the kingdomes of the world in a mo-
ment of time.
6 And the deuil said vnto him, All
this power will I giue thee, and the
glory of them ; for that is deliuered vnto
me, & to whomsoeuer I will, I giue it.
7 If thou therefore wilt ‖worship
me, all shalbe thine.
8 And Iesus answered and said vnto him, Get thee behinde me, Satan : for
it is written, Thou shalt worship the
Lord thy God; and him onely shalt

gogues, being [illegible] of all.
16 ¶ And hee [illegible] to *Nazareth, *Matt. 13. 54.
where he had bene [illegible]t vp, and as
his custome was, he [illegible] the Synagogue on the Sabbath [illegible] and
stood vp for to reade.
17 And there was deliuered [illegible]
him the booke of the Prophet E[illegible]
and when he had opened the Booke, he
found the place where it was written,
18 *The Spirit of the Lord is vpon *Esay 61. 1
mee, because hee hath anointed mee, to
preach the Gospel to the poore, he hath
sent mee to heale the broken hearted, to
preach deliuerance to the captiues, and
recouering of sight to the blinde, to set
at libertie them that are bruised,
19 To preach the acceptable yeere of
the Lord.
20 And he closed the booke, and hee
gaue it againe to the minister, and sate
downe : and the eyes of all them that
were in the Synagogue were fastened
on him.
21 And hee began to say vnto them,
This day is this Scripture fulfilled in
your eares.
22 And all bare him witnesse, and
wondered at the gracious wordes,
which proceeded out of his mouth. And
they said, Is not this Iosephs sonne?
23 And hee said vnto them, Yee will
surely say vnto me this prouerbe, Phy-
sition, heale thy selfe : Whatsoeuer wee
haue heard done in Capernaum, doe also here in thy countrey.
24 And hee said, Verely I say vnto

This is a picture from the 1611 King James Version Bible showing that there was no letter J in the 1611 KJV Version Bible

Here is proof that there was no letter J up until the 1700s. The name Jesus is simply a combination of the Latin and Greek IESOUS. Please note the similarity between the Greek IESOUS and pagan deity of Zeus. In fact, the pagan deity of Zeus is not pronounced in its original tongue as we read it. As I have said, there isn't even a letter or "J" sound in the Greek Alphabet. The Messiah did not speak English and neither did He speak Greek. The Messiah did not speak English and neither did He speak Greek. He spoke Hebrew and was from the Tribe of Judah as stated in Hebrews 7:14.

⋆12⋆

Pagan Birthdays

Birthdays are regarded and treated like a Holiday, but the truth of the matter is and the question is, are we instructed by the Word of The Most High God to be celebrating our Birthdays? Birthdays are the highest of all satanic holidays. Birthdays are not part of our heritage but a learned behavior that was given to us by the Gentiles and something we have embraced during our captivity. The Most High God told Jeremiah to tell the children of Israel not to fallow after the customs and traditions of the Gentiles (heathen), but we as a people (12 Tribes/Israel) are stiff necked and hard headed:

> **Jeremiah 10:2 Thus saith the LORD, Learn not the way of the heathen, and be not dismayed at the signs of heaven; for the heathen are dismayed at them.**

King Solomon tells us that a man's death is better that one's birth. This should let us know that your birthday is worthless in the eyesight of he Most High God:

Ecclesiastes 7:1 A good name is better than precious ointment; and the day of death than the day of one's birth.

We read in Job chapter 3 verses 1 through 6. Job cursed his born day/ Birthday. This should allow us to know that we shouldn't be celebrating our birthdays

Job 3:1-6 After this opened Job his mouth, and cursed his day.

2 And Job spake, and said,

3 Let the day perish wherein I was born, and the night in which it was said, There is a man child conceived.

4 Let that day be darkness; let not God regard it from above, neither let the light shine upon it.

5 Let darkness and the shadow of death stain it; let a cloud dwell upon let the blackness of the day terrify it.

6 As for that night, let darkness seize upon it; let it not be joined unto the days of the year, let it not come into the number of the months.

In 1969 Anton Lavey wrote The Satanic Bible, and on page 96 on the 1976 version, it mentions birthdays:

The highest of all holidays in the Satanic religion is the date of one's own birth. This is in direct contradiction to the holy of holy days of other religions, which deify a particular god who has been created in an anthropomorphic form of their own image, thereby showing that the ego is not really buried.

The Satanist feels: "Why not really be honest and if you are going to create a god in your image, why not create that god

as yourself." Every man is a god if he chooses to recognize himself as one. So, the Satanist celebrates his own birthday as the most important holiday of the year. After all, aren't you happier about the fact that you were born than you are about the birth of someone you have never even met? Or for that matter, aside from religious holidays, why pay higher tribute to the birthday of a president or to a date in history than we do to the day we were brought into this greatest of all worlds?

Despite the fact that some of us may not have been wanted, or at least were not particularly planned, we're glad, even if no one else is, that we're here! You should give yourself a pat on the back, buy yourself whatever you want, treat yourself like the king (or god) that you are, and generally celebrate your birthday with as much pomp and ceremony as possible.

The Origin of the Birthday Cake

The history of cakes and candles began in Ancient Greece. The Greeks made round cakes to honor Artemis, the goddess of the moon and the goddess of hunt. They often decorated it with either 1 lit candle or several to represent the glow of the moon. Overtime, other cultures began to make cakes and ate them for their taste, rather than to honor Artemis. Have you ever wondered who the first pyromaniac was to light a cake on fire? The Greeks were credited with putting candles on cakes to represent the glow of the moon. They also believed that the smoke from the lit candles carried their prayers and wishes to their Gods who lived in the skies. Today, many cultures place candles on cakes out of tradition, as well as superstition. Usually, the quantity of candles on a cake is representative to the age being celebrated. The superstition is to make a silent wish and blow out all the candles at one time so the wish comes true.

★ 13 ★

Gentile Salvation & Gentile Nations

In Acts chapter 10 which details the conversion of the Gentile Cornelius. Yes Cornelius was a Gentile. The word centurion means: *A Roman officer in command of a hundred men.* The centurion was the commander of a centuria ("group of one hundred men). Also we know Cornelius was a Gentile when in Acts 10:1 when it says "There was a certain man in Caesarea called Cornelius", Caesarea is a Roman capital of Palestine. Cornelius feared the Most High God (AHAYAH) the Holy one of Israel. The Most High sent Cornelius to an ordained Israelite, so he could be taught fully about him. You have to come to Israel to be taught about the Most High God (AHAYAH). Pray and Fast to the Most High God that he leads you to a natural Israelites so that they can teach you about his laws statues and commandments.

> **Acts 10:1-5 There was a certain man in Caesarea called Cornelius, a centurion of the band called the Italian band,**

2 A devout man, and one that feared God with all his house, which gave much alms to the people, and prayed to God alway.

3 He saw in a vision evidently about the ninth hour of the day an angel of God coming in to him, and saying unto him, Cornelius.

4 And when he looked on him, he was afraid, and said, What is it, Lord? And he said unto him, Thy prayers and thine alms are come up for a memorial before God.

5 And now send men to Joppa, and call for one Simon, whose surname is Peter:

To the righteous Gentiles who are reading this, and have had their eyes and hearts open to the truth. The story of Cornelius is a great example for you to follow.

Acts 10:21-38 Then Peter went down to the men which were sent unto him from Cornelius; and said, Behold, I am he whom ye seek: what is the cause wherefore ye are come?

22 And they said, Cornelius the centurion, a just man, and one that feareth God, and of good report among all the nation of the Jews, was warned from God by an holy angel to send for thee into his house, and to hear words of thee.

23 Then called he them in, and lodged them. And on the morrow Peter went away with them, and certain brethren from Joppa accompanied him.

24 And the morrow after they entered into Caesarea. And Cornelius waited for them, and had called together his kinsmen and near friends.

25 And as Peter was coming in, Cornelius met him, and fell down at his feet, and worshipped him.

26 But Peter took him up, saying, Stand up; I myself also am a man.

27 And as he talked with him, he went in, and found many that were come together.

28 And he said unto them, Ye know how that it is an unlawful thing for a man that is a Jew to keep company, or come unto one of another nation; but God hath shewed me that I should not call any man common or unclean.

29 Therefore came I unto you without gainsaying, as soon as I was sent for: I ask therefore for what intent ye have sent for me?

30 And Cornelius said, Four days ago I was fasting until this hour; and at the ninth hour I prayed in my house, and, behold, a man stood before me in bright clothing,

31 And said, Cornelius, thy prayer is heard, and thine alms are had in remembrance in the sight of God.

32 Send therefore to Joppa, and call hither Simon, whose surname is Peter; he is lodged in the house of [one] Simon a tanner by the sea side: who, when he cometh, shall speak unto thee.

33 Immediately therefore I sent to thee; and thou hast well done that thou art come. Now therefore are we all here present before God, to hear all things that are commanded thee of God.

34 Then Peter opened his mouth, and said, Of a truth I perceive that God is no respecter of persons:

35 But in every nation he that feareth him, and worketh righteousness, is accepted with him.

36 The word which God sent unto the children of Israel, preaching peace by Jesus Christ: (he is Lord of all:)

37 That word, I say, ye know, which was published throughout all Judaea, and began from Galilee, after the baptism which John preached;

38 How God anointed Jesus of Nazareth with the Holy Ghost and with power: who went about doing good, and healing all that were oppressed of the devil; for God was with him.

We read that, Cornelius is a just man and one who feared, prayed and believed in the Most High God, but he had to go to Peter the Israelite/Jew in order to be taught the word of the Most High God. An angel of the Most High God came to Cornelius and told him to go to Peter the Israelite/Jew and he will tell him what he ought to know. It is the Job of Israel to teach the world. This is why it is important for us to know who the true Israelites are today (the so-called Black Americans / Negroes). They have the word of the Most High God, and they are the holders of salvation. Romans 11:11 it said through our fall, the Israelites/Jews salvation was granted to the Gentiles to provoke us to jealousy. Yes Gentiles can obtain salvation.

> **Romans 11:11 I say then, Have they stumbled that they should fall? The Most High forbid: but rather through their fall salvation is come unto the Gentiles, for to provoke them to jealousy.**

Precepts to Romans 11:11:

> **Ezekiel 18:23 Have I any pleasure at all that the wicked should die? saith the Most High: and not that he should return from his ways, and live?**

> **Acts 13:46 Then Paul and Barnabas waxed bold, and said, It was necessary that the word of the Most High should first have been spoken to you: but seeing ye put it from you, and judge yourselves unworthy of everlasting life, lo, we turn to the Gentiles.**

In this verse we see that the Most High will give glory, honour, and peace, to every man that worketh good, to the Jews first and the Gentiles.

> **Romans 2:10 But glory, honour, and peace, to every man that worketh good, to the Jew first, and also to the Gentile:**

Why Gentiles must be taught by the True Jews (12 tribes)

Israel is the first fruit, and all the other nations (Gentiles) must be taught the truth by a true Jew. Israel has to know this truth first; they are the priest of the Most High. They are the ones who have to take the Word of the Most High God to the other nations (Gentiles). The word is to Israel first, but we must not turn away any Gentile who desires to know the truth, instead we are to teach them his (The Most High God) Laws, Statues, and Commandments.

Exodus 19:6 And ye shall be unto me a kingdom of priests, and an holy nation. These are the words which thou shalt speak unto the children of Israel.

In Exodus 19 verse 6 we see The Most High God telling the children of Israel, that, he would make them a kingdom of Priests. He made them a kingdom of Priest so that they can teach the whole world the truth about him (The Most High God), and his commandments, laws, and statues. In Matthew chapter 10 verse 6 he (Christ/Messiah) tells the 12 disciples "But go rather to the lost sheep of the house of Israel". Israel has to know this truth first, because they are the teachers, and the Christ (YASHAYAH) was on a mission from the Most High God to awaken and redeem the lost sheep of the house of Israel (12 Tribes).

Matthew 10:5-7 These twelve Jesus sent forth, and commanded them, saying, Go not into the way of the Gentiles, and into any city of the Samaritans enter ye not:

6 But go rather to the lost sheep of the house of Israel.

7 And as ye go, preach, saying, The kingdom ofheaven is at hand.

In Isaiah chapter 41 verses 8 and 9 it clearly states that the children of Israel (12 Tribes) are the servants of the Most High. They are instructed to go out into the world as priests and teach the Word to the Jews first then the Gentiles about the Most High God (AHAYAH).

Isaiah 41:8-9 But thou, Israel, art my servant, Jacob whom I have chosen, the seed of Abraham my friend.

9 Thou whom I have taken from the ends of the earth, and called thee from the chief men thereof, and said unto thee, Thou art my servant; I have chosen thee, and not cast thee away.

Gentile Nations

We must understand that the Gentiles can obtain salvation and it is the Hebrew Israelites (12 Tribes) duty to teach them, because salvation is of the Jews. I will explain this later on in the book. These are the Gentiles / Heathens:

> **Genesis 10:1-20 Now these are the generations of the sons of Noah, Shem, Ham, and Japheth: and unto them were sons born after the flood.**
>
> **2 The sons of Japheth; Gomer, and Magog, and Madai, and Javan, and Tubal, and Meshech, and Tiras.**
>
> **3 And the sons of Gomer; Ashkenaz, and Riphath, and Togarmah.**
>
> **4 And the sons of Javan; Elishah, and Tarshish, Kittim, and Dodanim.**
>
> **5 By these were the isles of the Gentiles divided in their lands; every one after his tongue, after their families, in their nations.**
>
> **6 And the sons of Ham; Cush, and Mizraim, and Phut, and Canaan.**
>
> **7 And the sons of Cush; Seba, and Havilah, and Sabtah, and Raamah, and Sabtecha: and the sons of Raamah; Sheba, and Dedan.**
>
> **8 And Cush begat Nimrod: he began to be a mighty one in the earth.**
>
> **9 He was a mighty hunter before the LORD: wherefore it is said, Even as Nimrod the mighty hunter before the LORD.**

10 And the beginning of his kingdom was Babel, and Erech, and Accad, and Calneh, in the land of Shinar.

11 Out of that land went forth Asshur, and builded Nineveh, and the city Rehoboth, and Calah,

12 And Resen between Nineveh and Calah: the same is a great city.

13 And Mizraim begat Ludim, and Anamim, and Lehabim, and Naphtuhim,

14 And Pathrusim, and Casluhim, (out of whom came Philistim,) and Caphtorim.

15 And Canaan begat Sidon his firstborn, and Heth,

16 And the Jebusite, and the Amorite, and the Girgasite,

17 And the Hivite, and the Arkite, and the Sinite,

18 And the Arvadite, and the Zemarite, and the Hamathite: and afterward were the families of the Canaanites spread abroad.

19 And the border of the Canaanites was from Sidon, as thou comest to Gerar, unto Gaza; as thou goest, unto Sodom, and Gomorrah, and Admah, and Zeboim, even unto Lasha.

20 These are the sons of Ham, after their families, after their tongues, in their countries, and in their nations.

Here are the Gentiles Nations by their Nationality in today's World.

Easu / Edom - So called **White Man**

Elam - So called **India**

Asshur - So called **Assyria**

Aram - So called **Syria**

Ishmael - So called **Arabs**

Moab - So called **Palenstine**

Ammon - So called **Japanese**

Cush - So called **Ethiopians**

Mizraim - So called **Egyptians**

Phut - So called **North Africa**

Canaan - So called **South Africans**

Gomer - So called **Turkey**

Magog - So called **Russian**

Javan -So called **Greek**

Ashkenaz -So called **German**

Tarshish -So called **Spanish**

Kittim -So called **Cyprus**

What should the Gentiles do once they accept this Truth

Gentiles who accepts the Truth about who the children of Israel (12 Tribes) can't boast against Israel, as many do today. This is one reason why the Gentiles can't understand prophecy. The majority of prophecy in scripture is related to Israel (12 Tribes), if you don't know Israel then you can't understand those prophecies. Paul spoke about the Gentiles being crafted in and boasting against Israel in Romans 11:13-27. The Gentiles can only be brought in through Israel.

> **Romans 11:13-27 For I speak to you Gentiles, inasmuch as I am the apostle of the Gentiles, I magnify mine office:**
>
> **14 If by any means I may provoke to emulation them which are my flesh, and might save some of them.**
>
> **15 For if the casting away of them be the reconciling of the world, what shall the receiving of them be, but life from the dead?**
>
> **16 For if the firstfruit be holy, the lump is also holy: and if the root be holy, so are the branches.**
>
> **17 And if some of the branches be broken off, and thou, being a wild olive tree, wert graffed in among them, and with them partakest of the root and fatness of the olive tree;**
>
> **18 Boast not against the branches. But if thou boast, thou bearest not the root, but the root thee.**
>
> **19 Thou wilt say then, The branches were broken off, that I might be graffed in.**

20 Well; because of unbelief they were broken off, and thou standest by faith. Be not highminded, but fear:

21 For if God spared not the natural branches, take heed lest he also spare not thee.

22 Behold therefore the goodness and severity of God: on them which fell, severity; but toward thee, goodness, if thou continue in his goodness: otherwise thou also shalt be cut off.

23 And they also, if they abide not still in unbelief, shall be graffed in: for God is able to graff them in again.

24 For if thou wert cut out of the olive tree which is wild by nature, and wert graffed contrary to nature into a good olive tree: how much more shall these, which be the natural branches, be graffed into their own olive tree?

25 For I would not, brethren, that ye should be ignorant of this mystery, lest ye should be wise in your own conceits; that blindness in part is happened to Israel, until the fulness of the Gentiles be come in.

26 And so all Israel shall be saved: as it is written, There shall come out of Sion the Deliverer, and shall turn away ungodliness from Jacob:

27 For this is my covenant unto them, when I shall take away their sins.

Paul was telling the gentiles in these verses, don't think just because the Most High God has granted you understanding of the Word, that Israel is no more good and you are in their place. You can't boast against Israel (12 Tribes) or think your better than them. As a

Gentile, you can't think you are higher and mightier than the true and real Jew. You may know a little Hebrew, know the true names of the Father and Son, all this is good, but you can't make yourself better than Israel (12 Tribes), Always remember Israel is the natural tree branches.

Gentiles who obtain salvation

Those Gentiles who follow the example of Cornelius and follow the Laws, statues, and commandments of the Most High God who have been taught by a real Jew (12 Tribes) will obtain salvation. In Isaiah 14:2, for those Gentiles who will obtain salvation, you will be servants and handmaids in the Kingdom of Heaven; these will be a righteous servitude.

> **Isaiah 14:1-2 For the Most High will have mercy on Jacob, and will yet choose Israel, and set them in their own land: and the strangers shall be joined with them, and they shall cleave to the house of Jacob.**
>
> **2 And the people shall take them, and bring them to their place: and the house of Israel shall possess them in the land of the Most High for servants and handmaids: and they shall take them captives, whose captives they were; and they shall rule over their oppressors.**

In Isaiah 60:10-11 we read that the Gentiles who make it in will also build up the Jews (12 Tribes) walls.

> **Isaiah 60:10-11 And the sons of strangers shall build up thy walls, and their kings shall minister unto thee: for in my wrath I smote thee, but in my favour have I had mercy on thee.**
>
> **11 Therefore thy gates shall be open continually; they shall not be shut day nor night; that men may bring**

unto thee the forces of the Gentiles, and that their kings may be brought.

Precept to Isaiah 60:10

Revelation 21:24 And the nations of them which are saved shall walk in the light of it: and the kings of the earth do bring their glory and honour into it.

Those Gentiles who don't want to acknowledge or tell the true Jews (12 Tribes) who they are nor keep the Laws, statues, and the commandments of the Most High God you will be destroyed.

Isaiah 60:12 For the nation and kingdom that will not serve thee shall perish; yea, those nations shall be utterly wasted.

★14★

NIV Bible

Today many churches (congregations) are now using the New International Version (NIV) and many believe it will replace the King James Version. We are seeing this come to pass at an alarming rate. In the NIV whole scriptures has been taken out as well as words and many more. The NAB - New American Bible (Roman Catholic Church) NWT - New world Translation (Jehovah's Witnesses) is in agreement with the NIV Bible. The owner (Rupert Murdoch) of the NIV owns a porn company as well. The NIV, is straight out of the pits of Hell. The man appointed to be the Chairman of the Old Testament Committee of the NIV Committee on Bible Translation, Dr. Marten Woudstra, was a homosexual. Also, Virginia Mollenkott, who worked as the stylistic editor for the translation, is a lesbian. If this is not convincing enough, then consider this, the parent company (Harper Collins) who publishes the NIV, also publishes The Joy of Gay Sex, and The Satanic Bible. It doesn't take a whole lot of common sense to figure this out folks. The NIV is evil and corrupt.

Why isn't the word "Sodomite" in the NIV Bible?

The reason why the word Sodomite isn't in the NIV Bible is because; there were homosexuals on the NIV translating committee. One such sodomite was Virginia Mollenkott. Another sodomite was the Chairman of the NIV Old Testament Committee! The name of the sodomite Dr. Marten H. Woudstra (he's dead now). The following quote was ascribed to Dr. Woudstra, Chairman of the NIV Old Testament Committee:

> "*There is nothing in the Old Testament that corresponds to homosexuality as we understand it today*"

Dr. Virginia Mollenkott, a literary critic on the NIV translation is an open homosexual. In theEpiscopal magazine, Witness (June 1991, pp. 20-23), she admits, "*My homosexuality always been a part of me.*" Is it any wonder why the word sodomite is not in the NIV? Look below and see what they replaced the word "sodomite" with:

> **Deuteronomy 23:17 There shall be no whore of the daughters of Israel, nor sodomite of the sons** – Authorized KJV Bible

> **Deuteronomy 23:17 No Israelite man or woman is to become a shrine prostitute.** – NIV Bible

> **1 Kings 14:24 And there were also sodomites in the land: and they did to all the abominations of the nations which the LORD cast out before the children Israel.** – Authorized KJV Bible

> **1 King 14:24 There were even male shrine prostitutes in the land; the people engaged in all the detestable practices of the nations the LORD had driven out before the Israelites.** – NIV Bible

1 Kings 15:12 And he took away the sodomites out of the land, and removed all the idols that his fathers had made. – Authorized KJV Bible

1 Kings 15:12 He expelled the male shrine prostitutes from the land and got rid of all the idols his fathers had made. – NIV Bible

1 Kings 22:46 And the remnant of the sodomites, which remained in the days of his father Asa, he took out of the land. – Authorized KJV Bible

1 Kings 22:46 He rid the land of the rest of the male shrine prostitutes who remained there even after the reign of his father Asa. – NIV Bible

2 Kings 23:7 And he brake down the houses of the sodomites, that were by the house of the LORD, where the women wove hangings for the grove. – Authorized KJV Bible

2 Kings 23:7 He also tore down the quarters of the male shrine prostitutes, which were in the in the temple of the LORD and where women did weaving for Asherah. – NIV Bible

The earth is given into the hand of the wicked (***Job 9:24***). We must understand that the god of this world who is satan, run this present world and the people at the top are his servants. The fact is that, the NIV and others like it or miss leading people. We must be very aware what we read and believe in because this is a spiritual battle between good and evil. We must rely on the Authorized KJV Bible only.

Proverbs 30:6 Add thou not unto his words, lest he reprove thee, and thou be found a liar.

Revelation 22:18-19 For I testify unto every man that heareth the words of the prophecy of this book, If any man shall add unto these things, God shall add unto him the plagues that are written in this book:

19 And if any man shall take away from the words of the book of this prophecy, God shall take away his part out of the book of life, and out of the holy city, and *from* the things which are written in this book.

★ 15 ★

Who Are The Hebrew Israelites?

The Bible gives us reliable evidence of the ancestry of the ancient Hebrew Israelites. The history of the Hebrew Israelites begins in Genesis 11:10 where the genealogy of Shem is recorded. The ancestry of the Hebrew Israelites stems from Abraham, who was a Hebrew Israelites, and black (Genesis 14:13). Although the Egyptians were a Black race, we must understand that they are from the descendants of Ham. In the tenth chapter of Genesis this can be proven. The Hebrew Israelites are a Holy nation and above all the other nations on the face of the earth. This is recorded in Deuteronomy chapter seven.

> ***Deuteronomy 7:6-8 For thou art an holy people unto the Lord thy God: the Lord thy God hath chosen thee to be a special people unto himself, above all people that are upon the face of the earth.***

7 The Lord did not set his love upon you, nor choose you, because ye were more in number than any people; for ye were the fewest of all people:

8 But because the Lord loved you, and because he would keep the oath which he had sworn unto your fathers, hath the Lord brought you out with a mighty hand, and redeemed you out of the house of bondmen, from the hand of Pharaoh king of Egypt.

The children of Israel are The Most High's chosen people. They hold the keys to salvation to those Gentiles who accept the truth about the God of Israel and his chosen people. During the time while the black Israelites were in Egypt, the black Egyptians enslaved them. I will talk more about this later on in the book. Jesus (Yashaya) was also a black man, although the white religious institution portrays him as white. The messiah was also a Jew from the tribe of Judah. This can be pointed out in this following scripture:

John 4:9-10 then saith the woman of Samaria unto him, How is it that thou, being a Jew, askest drink of me, which am a woman of Samaria? for the Jews have no dealings with the Samaritans.

10 Jesus answered and said unto her, If thou knewest the gift of God, and who it is that saith to thee, Give me to drink; thou wouldest have asked of him, and he would have given thee living water.

The women of Samaria said unto the Messiah, "How is it that thou, being a Jew, askest drink of me, which am a woman of Samaria? For the Jews have no dealings with the Samaritans". This shows us that the Messiah was a Jew, because the women said "How is it that thou, being a Jew," She clearly knew that the Messiah was a Jew. Also the word Jew comes from the tribe of Judah as I stated earlier in this chapter. By us identifying what Nationality the Messiah was we can now identify his color. According to the 12 tribes the tribe of Judah is the so called Negroes of America who are Black and from the seed of Abraham.

As I pointed out that the messiah was from the tribe of Judah and this can be shown in this scripture:

> ***Hebrews 7:14 For it is evident that our Lord sprang out of Juda: of which tribe Moses spake nothing concerning priesthood.***

The foregoing information substantiates that the Hebrew Israelites and the prophets of the Bible were all black. Also we must understand that the so called Negros of America isn't African-Americans, but decedents of the Ancient Hebrew Israelites. Also to point out that the Africans enslaved the Hebrew Israelites, I will show this later on in the book.

The Covenant Between the Most High and Abraham

The Most High makes a covenant with Abraham and his seed. This covenant is very important when you read about Esau and Jacob and how religious institution make Jacob look like the bad guy and make him look like he stole Esau birthright. It's very important to understand the covenant that the Most High God made with Abraham. Shem is the genealogy of the children of Israel as stated in (Genesis 10:11) where the genealogy of Shem is recorded. Abraham was a Hebrew Israelites and came from the genealogy of Shem, and this is pointed out in this scripture:

> ***Genesis 14:13 And there came one that had escaped, and told Abram the Hebrew; for he dwelt in the plain of Mamre the Amorite, brother of Eshcol, and brother of Aner: and these were confederate with Abram.***

In Chapter 15 the Most High God makes a covenant with Abraham. In Genesis 15:13 this is proof that the children of Israel (12 Tribes) are the Most High chosen people, and this also lets us know that Jacob had the promises already before Esau. Jacob comes from the seed of Abraham and Jacob is the father of the 12 Tribes which make up the children of Israel. The Most High said *"Know of a surety that thy seed shall be a stranger in a land that is not theirs, and shall serve them; and they shall afflict them four hundred years"*. This is pointed out in the following scriptures, read the precepts for understanding:

> ***Genesis 15:12-13 And when the sun was going down, a deep sleep fell upon Abram; and, lo, an horror of great darkness fell upon him.***
>
> ***13 And he said unto Abram, Know of a surety that thy seed shall be a stranger in a land that is not theirs, and shall serve them; and they shall afflict them four hundred years;***

Precept to Genesis 15:13:

> ***Exodus 1:1 Now these are the names of the children of Israel, which came into Egypt; every man and his household came with Jacob.***
>
> ***Exodus 1:11 Therefore they did set over them taskmasters to afflict them with their burdens. And they built for Pharaoh treasure cities, Pithom and Raamses.***
>
> ***Exodus 12:40 Now the sojourning of the children of Israel, who dwelt in Egypt, was four hundred and thirty years.***

In that same day the Most High made a covenant with Abraham to give his seed a land, this is shown in the following scriptures:

Genesis 15:18-21 In the same day the LORD made a covenant with Abram, saying, Unto thy seed have I given this land, from the river of Egypt unto the great river, the river Euphrates:

19 The Kenites, and the Kenizzites, and the Kadmonites,

20 And the Hittites, and the Perizzites, and the Rephaims

21 And the Amorites, and the Canaanites, and the Girgashites, and the Jebusites.

In Genesis 17 the Most High makes another covenant with him and tells him *"he will multiply thee exceedingly and he shall be a father of many nations (12 Tribes) and he also tells him that Kings shall come out of thee"*. The Most High promise Abraham that he would be the father of many nations, this will be done through the seed of Abraham, Isaac, and Jacob who is the father of the 12 Tribes. This can be shown in the following scriptures:

Genesis 17:1-9 And when Abram was ninety years old and nine, the LORD appeared to Abram, and said unto him, I am the Almighty God; walk before me, and be thou perfect.

2 And I will make my covenant between me and thee, and will multiply thee exceedingly.

3 And Abram fell on his face: and God talked with him, saying,

4 As for me, behold, my covenant is with thee, and thou shalt be a father of many nations.

5 Neither shall thy name any more be called Abram, but thy name shall be Abraham; for a father of many nations have I made thee.

6 And I will make thee exceeding fruitful, and I will make nations of thee, and kings shall come out of thee.

7 And I will establish my covenant between me and thee and thy seed after thee in their generations for an everlasting covenant, to be a God unto thee, and to thy seed after thee.

8 And I will give unto thee, and to thy seed after thee, the land wherein thou art a stranger, all the land of Canaan, for an everlasting possession; and I will be their God.

9 And God said unto Abraham, Thou shalt keep my covenant therefore, thou, and thy seed after thee in their generations.

In Genesis chapter 17 the Most High makes an everlasting covenant with Abraham's son who is Isaac and with his seed after him. This is shown in these scriptures:

Genesis 17:19-20 And God said, Sarah thy wife shall bear thee a son indeed; and thou shalt call his name Isaac: and I will establish my covenant with him for an everlasting covenant and with his seed after him.

20 And as for Ishmael, I have heard thee: Behold, I have blessed him, and will make him fruitful, and will multiply him exceedingly; twelve princes shall he beget, and I will make him a great nation.

In Genesis chapter 21 Sarah conceived and had Isaac, this pointed out in these scriptures:

Genesis 21:2-3 For Sarah conceived, and bare Abraham a son in his old age, at the set time of which God had spoken to him.

3 And Abraham called the name of his son that was born unto him, whom Sarah bare to him, Isaac.

This covenant that the father made with Abraham is very important when understanding Esau and Jacob fight over the birthright in the womb, and understanding how Jacob already had the promises.

Esau and Jacob

Isaac's wife Rebekah conceives and has Esau and Jacob. According to the Bible you are what your father is (Ezra 2:59.) The Most High said "*Two nations are in thy womb, and two manner of people shall be separated from thy bowels*". Nation is short for Nationality. They weren't identical twins. The Most high speaks to Rebekah in this manner:

Genesis 25:21-34 And Isaac intreated the LORD for his wife, because she was barren: and the LORD was intreated of him, and Rebekah his wife conceived.

22 And the children struggled together within her; and she said, If it be so, why am I thus? And she went to enquire of the LORD.

23 And the LORD said unto her, Two nations are in thy womb, and two manner of people shall be separated from thy bowels; and the one people shall be stronger than the other people; and the elder shall serve the younger.

24 And when her days to be delivered were fulfilled, behold, there were twins in her womb.

25 And the first came out red, all over like an hairy garment; and they called his name Esau.

26 And after that came his brother out, and his hand took hold on Esau's heel; and his name was called Jacob: and Isaac was threescore years old when she bare them.

27 And the boys grew: and Esau was a cunning hunter, a man of the field; and Jacob was a plain man, dwelling in tents.

28 And Isaac loved Esau, because he did eat of his venison: but Rebekah loved Jacob.

29 And Jacob sod pottage: and Esau came from the field, and he was faint:

30 And Esau said to Jacob, Feed me, I pray thee, with that same red pottage; for I am faint: therefore was his name called Edom.

31 And Jacob said, Sell me this day thy birthright.

32 And Esau said, Behold, I am at the point to die: and what profit shall this birthright do to me?

33 And Jacob said, Swear to me this day; and he sware unto him: and he sold his birthright unto Jacob.

34 Then Jacob gave Esau bread and pottage of lentiles; and he did eat and drink, and rose up, and went his way: thus Esau despised his birthright.

In Verse 23 it says one "one people shall be stronger than the other people", meaning you would have one people more physically strong and spiritually strong. According to Genesis 15:13 this lets us know that the promise was already given to Jacob because Jacob is from Shem and Jacob is the Father of the 12 Tribes who will sojourn in that strange land, which is Egypt. Esau is the father of the Edomites you can read this in Genesis 36:1-43. That's why in Genesis 25:23 it said "Two nations are in thy womb, and two manner of people shall be separated from thy bowels". Then it goes on to say in verse 25 "And the first came out red, all over like an hairy garment; and they called his name Esau." It says red because the blood show forth through the skin and in today's society that would be the Europeans or what we call the White Caucasian. There is no such thing as Black people, Black is a color, but there is such a thing as Brown people like unto the color of the ground. And there is no such thing as white people; White is a color like the color of white printing paper. Esau was one of the sons of Isaac and the first born, meaning the first one that came out. In Genesis 25:23 it said that the elder would serve the younger brother, this lets us know that the promise was already given to Jacob before he was born. Jacob is the son of the promise and he is the one that the Most High promised that Esau would serve, that's why they were fighting in the womb. In 2 Esdras chapter six it tells us that Esau is the end of the world and Jacob is the beginning of the one that follows it. At the end of the world, meaning the end times which we are in. Esau is the end of the world. Meaning we will rule forever. You must ask yourself this, who is over the world today, what Nationality or group of people? It's the White Caucasian. Here are the scripture to prove this:

> ***2 Esdras 6:8-9*** **And he said unto me, From Abraham unto Isaac, when Jacob and Esau were born of him, Jacob's hand held first the heel of Esau.**
>
> ***9*** **For Esau is the end of the world, and Jacob is the beginning of it that followeth.—** *Authorized KJV Apocrypha*

12 Tribes

Jacob fathered 12 sons (Genesis 49:1-28). They are the ancestors of the tribes of Israel, and the ones for whom the tribes are named. The sons of Joseph, Ephraim and Manasseth, were given the status of independent tribes. Each occupied a separate territory (Numbers 34:1-29), except the tribe of Levi, which was set apart to serve in the Holy Temple (Numbers 18:24). These are the 12 Tribes of Israel:

Reuben, Simeon, Levi, Judah, Zebulon, Issachar, Gad, Asher, Napthali, Ephraim, Manasseth, Benjamin. At this point, I would like to explain to the readers that Jerusalem was the birthplace of us all (Galatians 4:26). The 12 Tribes of Israel today can be identified as the following:

Reuben—So called Seminole Indians/Aboriginal Australians

Simeon—So called Dominicans

Levi—So called Haitians

Judah—So called African Americans/Negroes

Zebulon—Guatemalans/Panamanians **Issachar**—So called Mexicans

Gad—So called North American Indians

Asher—Columbians/Brazilians/Argentines/ Venezuelans **Napthali**—Hawaiians/Samoans/Tongans/ Fijians **Ephraim**—So called Puerto Ricans

Manasseth—So called Cubans

Benjamin—So called Jamaicans/Trinidadians/Guyanese

The 12 Tribes of Israel are the Most High people forever. This is shown in these scriptures:

> ***I Chronicles 17:21-22 And what one nation in the earth is like thy people Israel, whom God went to redeem to be his own people, to make thee a name of greatness and terribleness, by driving out nations from before thy people, whom thou hast redeemed out of Egypt.***
>
> ***22 For thy people Israel didst thou make thine own people for ever; and thou, LORD, becamest their God.***

The Color Of The Hebrew Israelites

For years, scholars, theologians and archaeologist have debated the answer to the question, "How did the ancient Hebrew Israelites people look physically? My research has lead me to confirm that although the scriptures and other historical documents have left a lot of evidence that confirms the physical appearance of the Hebrew Israelites people. Most religious institutions teach that the people in Israel today known as "Ashkenazi Jews or Jewish People" are the direct descendants of the ancient Israelites, because they proclaim themselves to be the real Jews. The people today over in Israel are not the real Jews neither do they look like the Hebrew Israelites (children of Israel), they are white Europeans. The Europeans had a reason to lie and to cover up the truth to develop a white supremacy. They lied about the truth about how the Hebrew Israelites looked like, when they made it illegal for a black man and women to learn how to read during slavery times. They knew how holy the children of Israel were. I will talk more about the Jewish people and who they are further in the book.

The Bible tells us and shows us the color of the Hebrew Israelites. Many will argue up and down or say that color doesn't matter when it really does. We didn't make it a color issue the white Europeans made it one when they started to paint all the images white during the renaissance period. The Bible is a history book of the children of Israel. Throughout scripture Israel is described as physically looking like the sons of Ham in appearance. Ham was one of Noah's three sons, Shem and Japheth were the other two (Genesis 9:18). Noah's descendants repopulated the earth after the Great Flood. Ham's descendants are traced to the families of Africa. Ham in Hebrew means Black, hot and burnt. Egypt was traditionally called "the Land of Ham," and Ham was considered to be the ancestor of the Egyptians and of all African peoples south of Egypt. The Hebrew Israelites are descendants of Noah son Shem, through Abraham; he is the father of the Hebrew Israelite Nation. Abraham is the father of Isaac, Isaac is the father of Jacob, Jacob had twelve sons and these sons are the progenitors of the Israelite nation.

Joseph was one of the twelve sons of Jacob. Jacob sired Joseph in his old age, and he was clearly his favorite son. This caused Joseph's brothers to become jealous of him. Their jealousy resulted in Joseph being sold by Arab merchants as a slave to Egyptians (Genesis 37:3-36). Joseph became governor of Egypt and was second in command to Pharaoh in authority (Genesis 41:40-41 and Genesis 42:6). There was a famine in Canaan, where Jacob and his sons lived. Pharaoh had a dream which Joseph interpreted. His dream told of the forthcoming famine and gave Egypt an opportunity to prepare by storing food.) So, Jacob sent his ten sons to Egypt to buy bread. When Joseph's ten brothers came into Egypt they were brought before him. Joseph recognized his brothers, but they didn't recognize him, this can be pointed out in the following scriptures:

> ***Genesis 42:1-8 now when Jacob saw that there was corn in Egypt, Jacob said unto his sons, Why do ye look one upon another?***
>
> ***2 And he said, Behold, I have heard that there is corn in Egypt: get you down thither, and buy for us from thence; that we may live, and not die.***
>
> ***3 And Joseph's ten brethren went down to buy corn in Egypt.***
>
> ***4 But Benjamin, Joseph's brother, Jacob sent not with his brethren; for he said, Lest peradventure mischief befall him.***
>
> ***1 And the sons of Israel came to buy corn among those that came: for the famine was in the land of Canaan.***
>
> ***2 And Joseph was the governor over the land, and he it was that sold to all the people of the land: and Joseph's brethren came, and bowed down themselves before him with their faces to the earth.***
>
> ***3 And Joseph saw his brethren, and he knew them, but made himself strange unto them, and spake roughly unto them; and he said unto them, Whence come ye? And they said, From the land of Canaan to buy food.***

4 And Joseph knew his brethren, but they knew not him.

Since the ancient Egyptians were a black people, Joseph had to be black also. Joseph brothers would have recognized him easily among the "black" Egyptians. But Joseph's own flesh and blood brothers thought he was an Egyptian. Scripture tells us that Moses killed an Egyptian, after he saw him mistreating a Hebrew Israelite. So Moses had to flee from the land of Egypt for his life, because Pharaoh found out and sought to kill him. Pharaoh was trying to kill Moses because he found out Moses was a Hebrew and not his flesh and blood grandson (Exodus 2:12-15). Moses fled to the land of Midian (located in Saudi Arabia) where he helped seven daughters of the priest of Midian water their flock, after chasing away some bully shepherds. The girls went home to their father, Reuel and told him what happened:

Exodus 2:16-19 Now the priest of Midian had seven daughters: and they came and drew water, and filled the troughs to water their father's flock.

17 And the shepherds came and drove them away: but Moses stood up and helped them, and watered their flock.

18 And when they came to Reuel their father, he said, How is it that ye are come so soon to day?

19 And they said, An Egyptian delivered us out of the hand of the shepherds, and also drew water enough for us, and watered the flock.

Notice they didn't say a Hebrew in Egyptian clothing saved us; they described Moses as a black-skinned descendant of Ham (Egyptian). Further proof that Moses was "black" can be found in Exodus 4:6-7, in this passage, AHAYAH, (The Creator's name in Hebrew) is showing Moses a miracle so that he can prove to the children of Israel who sent him. This can be shown in these scriptures:

Exodus 4:6 And the LORD said furthermore unto him, Put now thine hand into thy bosom. And he put his hand into his bosom: and when he took it out, behold, his hand was leprous as snow.

7 And he said, Put thine hand into thy bosom again. And he put his hand into his bosom again; and plucked it out of his bosom, and, behold, it was turned again as his other flesh.

In verse 7 it says, The Lord told Moses to put his hand back into his bosom, and it turned as his other flesh. Meaning that the rest of his body (skin) was other than white or the opposite of white, which is black. Also notice in verse 6 when the Most High turned Moses hand to leprous as snow, and we all know that the color of snow is white. Then he turns his skin back again to his other (own) flesh which was black. Moses was a Hebrew Israelites from the tribe of Levi. This also shows us that Paul was mistaken for an Egyptian, although they were Black, they weren't from Shem as the Israelites were.)

★ 16 ★

Identifying The 12 Tribes of Israel

Greetings to the 12 Tribes of Israel who are scattered throughout the four corners of the World. It's important to identify the 12 tribes of Israel today, because these are the Most High chosen people. They have been enslaved and scattered throughout the four corners of the earth. Both their land and identity have been stolen in one of the biggest conspiracies in the history of mankind. Wars are being fought (physically, spiritually, mentally, and financially); the earth's resources are intentionally being destroyed; all in an attempt to prevent the rise of these people. The religious and educational sectors of government will not share this information with you.

> **1 Chronicles 17:21-22 And what one nation in the earth is like thy people Israel, whom the Most High went to redeem to be his own people, to make thee a name of greatness and terribleness, by driving out nations from before thy people, whom thou hast redeemed out of Egypt?**

22 For thy people Israel didst thou make thine own people for ever; and thou, LORD, becamest their God. - ***Authorized KJV Bible***

Northern Kingdom and Southern Kingdom

The Northern Kingdom consists of the so-called "Native Indian" tribes who predominately came to the Americas around 718 B.C. after serving in the Assyrian captivity. These are the indigenous people of North, Central, and South America along with Canada and the Caribbean islands. The Northern Kingdom Tribes are:

- Asher
- Ephraim
- Manasseh
- Gad
- Issachar
- Naphtali
- Reuben
- Simeon
- Zebulun

2 Esdras 13:39-47 And whereas thou sawest that he gathered another peaceable multitude unto him;

40 Those are the ten tribes, which were carried away prisoners out of their own land in the time of Osea the king, whom Salmanasar the king of Assyria led away captive, and he carried them over the waters, and so came they into another land.

41 But they took this counsel among themselves, that they would leave the multitude of the heathen, and go forth into a further country, where never mankind dwelt,

42 That they might there keep their statutes, which they never kept in their own land.

43 And they entered into Euphrates by the narrow places of the river.

44 For the most High then shewed signs for them, and held still the flood, till they were passed over.

45 For through that country there was a great way to go, namely, of a year and a half: and the same region is called Arsareth.

46 Then dwelt they there until the latter time; and now when they shall begin to come,

47 The Highest shall stay the springs of the stream again, that they may go through: therefore sawest thou the multitude with peace. – *Authorized KJV Apocrypha*

Southern Kingdom

The Southern Kingdom consist of the so-called "Negro" tribes of the Nation of Israel, who predominately came from the coast of the West Africa to America and the Caribbean islands by way of cargo slave ships, which can be read in Deuteronomy 28:68. If you look in the areas of Liberia, Ghana, Nigeria, Timbuktu, Ethiopia & Egypt, a large population of Judah, Benjamin and Levi still exist in these areas today. The Southern Kingdom Tribes are:

- Benjamin
- Judah
- Levi

Identifying the Sons of Jacob

Reuben

The book of Genesis describes Reuben as Jacob's strength and might due to fact that he was the firstborn of the twelve tribes please read Genesis 49:3. Reuben's dignity and power describes the honorable spirit that he possessed which refrained him from signing any treaties with the European (Esau) settlers. Unstable as water describes the nomadic lifestyles that are led by the other sons of Reuben who are Australia's Aboriginal tribes. This is also in reference to the Aboriginal Australians who still till this day lives a very primitive lifestyle.

> **Genesis 49:3-4 Reuben, thou art my firstborn, my might, and the beginning of my strength, the excellency of dignity, and the excellency of power:**
>
> **4 Unstable as water, thou shalt not excel; because thou wentest up to thy father's bed; then defiledst thou it: he went up to my couch.**

People: Seminole Indians / Aboriginal Australians
Location: Florida and Australia surrounding areas. Also scattered throughout the World.
Characteristics: Reuben must guard their Thoughts

Simeon

The Scripture says that instruments of cruelty are in the habitation of Simeon. This is in reference to the religious practices (Santeria) of the so-called Dominicans, which are heavily influenced by voodoo. Simeon and his brother Levi are mentioned as being partakers in voodoo, which a form of black magic. Jacob then states that his sons Simeon and Levi would be divided in Jacob. Though Simeon and Levi live on the same exact island and deal with the same exact religious practices, they can't seem to get along one with the other. Simeon is one of the 10 tribes who after the Assyrian captivity, set shore to the Americas which can be read in 2 Kings 17:17-41 and 2 Esdras 13:39-47

> **Genesis 49:5-7 Simeon and Levi are brethren; instruments of cruelty are in their habitations**
>
> **6 O my soul, come not thou into their secret; unto their assembly, mine honour, be not thou united: for in their anger they slew a man, and in their selfwill they digged down a wall.**
>
> **7 Cursed be their anger, for it was fierce; and their wrath, for it was cruel: I will divide them in Jacob, and scatter them in Israel.**

People: Dominicans
Location: Dominican Republic surrounding areas. Also scattered throughout the World.
Characteristics: Simeon, take heed the spirit of deceit and of envy

Levi

Simeon and Levi are brethren. Although all the twelve sons of Jacob are brethren, Simeon and Levi would both together inhabit the same island in the last days. The same prophecies that fell upon Simeon are also used to describe the conditions of Levi, Voodoo is also prevalent amongst the so-called Haitians. This is what the bible means by instruments of cruelty in the habitation of Levi. Levi was not counted as a tribe of Israel, but they were separated to perform the duty of priesthood, which can be read in Numbers 18:2-4, and Deuteronomy 19:9-11. Levi eventually fell from the priesthood and became as one of the tribes of Israel Malachi 2:1-9. You may read more information on Levi from a book called Babylon to Timbuktu on page 84 & 90.

> **Genesis 49:5-7 Simeon and Levi are brethren; instruments of cruelty are in their habitations**

6 O my soul, come not thou into their secret; unto their assembly, mine honour, be not thou united: for in their anger they slew a man, and in their selfwill they digged down a wall.

7 Cursed be their anger, for it was fierce; and their wrath, for it was cruel: I will divide them in Jacob, and scatter them in Israel.

People: Haitians
Location: Haiti and the surrounding areas. Also scattered throughout the World.
Characteristics: Levi must come back to the Priesthood and must not be arrogance in knowing their Holy position.

Judah

Judah would be praised based on the fact that our Lord and Saviour of Israel (Christ/Messiah) would come from Judah in Hebrews 7:14. Judah is described as being a young lion that has crouched down like an old lion; one of the questions we must ask is who or what will rouse him up? Once Judah rises, the rest of the tribes will come following after. Judah is one of the most successful in athletics, business, inventions, entertainment, etc. This is prophecy which can be read in Deuteronomy 33:7 which state that the Most High would make his hands sufficient for him (edom). The king ship of the Israel was established with the tribe of Judah, and is an everlasting king ship with no end, because Christ/Messiah is both King and Priest after the order of Melchizedek, please read Acts 2:29-30, Psalms 110:4, and Hebrews 7:1. To find more information on Judah please read a book called from Babylon to Timbuktu on page 84, and 90.

Genesis 49:8-12 Judah, thou art he whom thy brethren shall praise: thy hand shall be in the neck of thine enemies; thy father's children shall bow down before thee.

9 Judah is a lion's whelp: from the prey, my son, thou art gone up: he stooped down, he couched as a lion, and as an old lion; who shall rouse him up?

10 The sceptre shall not depart from Judah, nor a lawgiver from between his feet, until Shiloh come; and unto him shall the gathering of the people be.

11 Binding his foal unto the vine, and his ass's colt unto the choice vine; he washed his garments in wine, and his clothes in the blood of grapes: 12 His eyes shall be red with wine, and his teeth white with milk.

People: African Americans / Negroes
Location: United States of America and the surround areas. Also scattered throughout the World.
Characteristics: Judah must be careful of Fortitude, and Love of Money, and Fornication.

Zebulon

The habitation of Zebulun borders the Atlantic and Pacific Ocean, making it a haven of ships. Zebulon according to the Bible would "rejoice in his going out". When you examine the land of Zebulon, he is surrounded by his brethren of the tribes of Israel. Murder and Disease such as smallpox went throughout Guatamala all the way through Panama during the early 16th century under the hand of the Spaniards. The Bible prophesied that Israel would be overtaken and consumed by pestilence, disease, and murder in Deuteronomy 28:21-22; 25.

Genesis 49:13 Zebulun shall dwell at the haven of the sea; and he shall be for an haven of ships; and his border shall be unto Zidon.

People: Guatemalans / Panamanians

Location: Guatemaia and Panama surrounding areas. Also scattered throughout the World.

Characteristics: Zebulun must show and have more Compassion and Mercy

Issachar

The Bible identifies the so-called Mexican as a strong ass couching between two burdens which denote his great physical strength. Siesta is an essential part of Mexican culture, and is defined when Jacob states they saw that rest was good. Issachar is also known throughout the Americas for physical hard labor and is called by his father Jacob a servant unto tribute in Genesis 49:15.

> **Genesis 49:14-15 Issachar is a strong ass couching down between two burdens:**
>
> **15 And he saw that rest was good, and the land that it was pleasant; and bowed his shoulder to bear, and became a servant unto tribute.**

People: Mexicans

Location: Mexico and surrounding areas. Also scattered throughout the World.

Characteristics: Issachar must not turn from their simplicity

Gad

Gad is a part of the 10 lost Tribes of Israel. If you look at some of the city names in America, especially in the North, like (Utah, Ohio, Dakota, and Kansas, etc. Gad was the original inhabitants of these states, but also ask yourself this, Why isn't that the Native Americans don't own the United States? If you go back to Genesis 49:19 it says "a troop shall overcome him", that troop is the U.S. Calvary. Many Atrocities have been committed against Gad, similar to that of the Native Indians of Central and South America. The Bible even describes the physical facial features of Gad, stating that their "faces were like the faces of lions" mentioned in 1 Chronicles 12:8.

Genesis 49:19 Gad, a troop shall overcome him: but he shall overcome at the last.

People: North American Indians
Location: United States and the surrounding areas. Also scattered throughout the World.
Characteristics: Gad must take heed of hatred

Asher

The children of Asher can be found in the oil rich countries of South America. As Jacob told his son, "Let him dip his foot in oil". Like many of the tribes who reside in Central, South America and the Caribbean Islands, the land of Asher is blessed with many resources and delicacies as Genesis 49:20 states

Genesis 49:20 Out of Asher his bread shall be fat, and he shall yield royal dainties.

People: Brazilians / Argentines / Venezuelans
Location: South America and surrounding areas. Also scattered throughout the World.
Characteristics: Asher must be careful of being two faced of vice and Virtue

Naphtali

Naphtali according to Bible prophecy would inhabit the South Seas (Hebrew translation Yam=Seas; Due 33:23). Naphtali is also identified as a people "satisfied with favour". As you can see, the children of Naphtali are a very beautiful people. Hawaiian culture still contains many Hebrew customs, circumcision being the most notable.

> **Genesis 49:21 Naphtali is a hind let loose: he giveth goodly words.**

People: Hawaiians / Samoans / Tongans / Fijians
Location: Hawaii, New Zealand, and Fiji surrounding areas. Also scattered throughout the World.
Characteristics: Naphtali must maintain their natural Goodness

Ephraim

Joseph, son of Jacob, bore two sons during his time in Egypt please read Genesis 41:50-52 and Genesis 46:20. Ephraim and Manasseh received the blessing of Reuben if you read 1 Chronicles 5:1-2, which in turn caused them to be adopted as one of the son of Jacob read Genesis the 48th chapter. The archers who grieved the children of Joseph are Spaniards and conquistadors who through genocide wiped out a large portion of Ephraim's population. Ephraim and Manasseh, like many of their brethren were bless with fertile, tropical land.

> **Genesis 49:22-26 Joseph is a fruitful bough, even a fruitful bough by a well; whose branches run over the wall:**
>
> **23 The archers have sorely grieved him, and shot at him, and hated him: 24 But his bow abode in strength, and the arms of his hands were made strong by the hands of the mighty God of Jacob; (from thence is the shepherd, the stone of Israel:)**
>
> **25 Even by the God of thy father, who shall help thee; and by the Almighty, who shall bless thee with blessings of heaven above, blessings of the deep that lieth under, blessings of the breasts, and of the womb: 26 The blessings of thy father have prevailed above the blessings of my progenitors unto the utmost bound of the everlasting hills: they shall be on the head of**

Joseph, and on the crown of the head of him that was separate from his brethren.

People: Puerto Ricans
Location: Puerto Rico and the surrounding areas. Also scattered throughout the World.
Characteristics: Ephraim must follow after Sobriety

Manasseh

Joseph, son of Jacob, bore two sons during his time in Egypt please read Genesis 41:50-52 and Genesis 46:20. Ephraim and Manasseh received the blessing of Reuben if you read 1 Chronicles 5:1-2, which in turn caused them to be adopted as one of the son of Jacob read Genesis the 48th chapter. The archers who grieved the children of Joseph are Spaniards and conquistadors who through genocide wiped out a large portion of Ephraim's population. Ephraim and Manasseh, like many of their brethren were bless with fertile, tropical land.

Genesis 49:22-26 Joseph is a fruitful bough, even a fruitful bough by a well; whose branches run over the wall:

23 The archers have sorely grieved him, and shot at him, and hated him: 24 But his bow abode in strength, and the arms of his hands were made strong by the hands of the mighty God of Jacob; (from thence is the shepherd, the stone of Israel:)

25 Even by the God of thy father, who shall help thee; and by the Almighty, who shall bless thee with blessings of heaven above, blessings of the deep that lieth under, blessings of the breasts, and of the womb:
26 The blessings of thy father have prevailed above the blessings of my progenitors unto the utmost bound of the everlasting hills: they shall be on the head of

Joseph, and on the crown of the head of him that was separate from his brethren.

People: Cubans
Location: Cuba and surrounding areas. Also scattered throughout the World.
Characteristics: Manasseh must follow after Sobriety

Benjamin

Benjamin, they are described by their father Jacob as having the spirit of a wolf. Wolves are known for howling at the moon, similar to the way that the so-called West Indian sings songs Zion towards the heavens. Under the Maroons, Benjamin would overtake the slave ships and turn them back towards the coast of West Africa. The Bible also tells us that the land is blessed in which Benjamin dwells, "The beloved of the Lord shall dwell in safety by him; and the Lord shall cover him all the day long, and he shall dwell between his shoulders". For more information on Benjamin, please read From Babylon to Timbuktu on page 84, 90.

Genesis 49:27 Benjamin shall ravin as a wolf: in the morning he shall devour the prey, and at night he shall divide the spoil.

People: Jamaicans / Trinidadians / Guyanese
Location: Jamaica and the surrounding areas. Also scattered throughout the World.
Characteristics: Benjamin must be mindful to have a pure mind

★ 17 ★

The Curse

The so called Black people of America are the true descendants of the Ancient Hebrew Israelites mentioned in the Bible. I also find that the curses mentioned in the Bible refer directly to the Blacks in America today and the 12 Tribes of Israel. The children of Israel were the chosen people of the Most High and were chosen to be a light to the Gentiles, but they were a rebellious nation. The scripture tells us to show his people (children of Israel) their transgression and the house of Jacob their sins. Here are some scripture that depicts the behavior of the children of Israel:

> ***Hosea 4:6 My people are destroyed for lack of knowledge: because thou hast rejected knowledge, I will also reject thee, that thou shalt be no priest to me: seeing thou hast forgotten the law of thy God, I will also forget thy children.***

It's said "My people are destroyed for lack of knowledge. Notice it says my people, that people or nation is the 12 Tribes or the children of Israel. This can be proven in *Exodus 3:10*. They have been cut off by the Most High because we lack knowledge. They lack knowledge of the God of Israel who saved their forefather from the Egyptians. That's why in today's society their children are lost majority of their young teenagers are in jail and that's because the Most High has forgotten their children. The children of Israel have forgotten the law of the Most High that he gave unto their forefathers. Today in these so called Churches they preach we don't have to keep the law and that it's done away with, that's a lie, and we are to keep the laws of the Most High forever.

> ***Zechariah 7:11-12 But they refused to hearken, and pulled away the shoulder, and stopped their ears, that they should not hear.***
>
> ***12 Yea, they made their hearts as an adamant stone, lest they should hear the law, and the words which the Lord of hosts hath sent in his spirit by the former prophets: therefore came a great wrath from the Lord of hosts.***

Notice it said they. In today's society getting the children of Israel to understand who they are and their true Nationality is nearly impossible. When someone tries to present this truth to the 12 tribes by telling them who they are and that cargo slave ships are mentioned in the bible they will immediately cut you off and turn away their shoulder, stop their ears from hearing, and keep on walking. That's why it goes on to say "they made their hearts as an adamant stone" meaning they have harden their hearts. They refuse to hear his laws and the Most High words which he sent by his spirit by the former prophets, that's why it goes on to say "therefore came a great wrath from the Most High of hosts". This is why you see the children of Israel at the bottom. Majority of them are in jail, and many of them have diseases like high blood pressure, and many more. Continue to read Zechariah 7:13-14.

> ***Ezekiel 2:3-5 And he said unto me, Son of man, I send thee to the children of Israel, to a rebellious nation that hath rebelled against me: they and their fathers have transgressed against me, even unto this very day.***

4 For they are impudent children and stiffhearted. I do send thee unto them; and thou shalt say unto them, Thus saith the Lord GOD.

5 And they, whether they will hear, or whether they will forbear, (for they are a rebellious house,) yet shall know that there hath been a prophet among them.

The Hebrew Israelites are a rebellious people. Just look at the so called Blacks and the other 12 tribes today. You have children cursing out their parents; the children are over their parents it's just all out of order. The children of Israel have rebelled against the Father and have violated his laws until this very day. So why in these so called churches they teach that the Most High people don't have to keep the law? That is a lie; they are to keep the law as I already mentioned. They are disrespectful children as a nation.

Because of their disobedience, the Most High scattered the children of Israel throughout the different parts of the world and brought evil against them, this is foretold in the prophecies of the Holy Scripture. All the curses are to fit the Jews who are the so called Negros or what society calls the African-American and the 12 Tribes. I will explain the curse that fell upon the children of Israel mentioned in Deuteronomy chapter 28 below:

Deuteronomy 28:15 But it shall come to pass, if thou wilt not hearken unto the voice of the LORD thy God, to observe to do all his commandments and his statutes which I command thee this day; that all these curses shall come upon thee, and overtake thee:

Deuteronomy 28:16 Cursed shalt thou be in the city, and cursed shalt thou be in the field.

If you look at any "inner city" in the United States, you will find death and destruction like nowhere else. Many of these cities look like they belong in any war-torn country, they're devastated. These cities are largely populated by "African Americans", as this is where the majority of "blacks" in the United States live. Wherever you find a large population of "Blacks" living in rural/country areas, you will find the same death and destruction like you find in the urban city areas.

> ***Deuteronomy 28:17 Cursed shall be thy basket and thy store.***

> ***Deuteronomy 28:18 Cursed shall be the fruit of thy body, and the fruit of thy land, the increase of thy kine, and the flocks of thy sheep.***

These curses are going to follow the so-called "Blacks", for as long as they continue to sin against the Most High.

> ***Deuteronomy 28:20 The LORD shall send upon thee cursing, vexation, and rebuke, in all that thou settest thine hand unto for to do, until thou be destroyed, and until thou perish quickly; because of the wickedness of thy doings, whereby thou hast forsaken me.***

Just about everything "African Americans" have tried to do to improve their living conditions as a people, has failed. They have tried the political system (voting), the educational system (attaining college degrees), and economics (capitalism). But all these genres have been useless to them.

> ***Deuteronomy 28:21 The LORD shall make the pestilence cleave unto thee, until he have consumed thee from off the land, whither thou goest to possess it.***

> ***Deuteronomy 28:22 The LORD shall smite thee with a consumption, and with a fever, and with an inflammation, and with an extreme burning, and with the sword, and with blasting, and with mildew; and they shall pursue thee until thou perish.***

Verse 22 is referring to diseases and lynching (killings). One of the worst episodes, of the life of a slave was the middle passage, the voyage from West Africa to America. The conditions on the slave ships were unbearable; two to four hundred captives were packed like sardines in the bottom of the ships.

> ***Deuteronomy 28:23 And thy heaven that is over thy head shall be brass, and the earth that is under thee shall be iron***

> ***Deuteronomy 28:24 The LORD shall make the rain of thy land powder and dust: from heaven shall it come down upon thee, until thou be destroyed.***

> ***Deuteronomy 28:25 The LORD shall cause thee to be smitten before thine enemies: thou shalt go out one way against them, and flee seven ways before them: and shalt be removed into all the kingdoms of the earth***

In verse 25 it *clearly* tells us that Israel (12 Tribes) is to be smitten/ defeated by their enemies. Also In verse 25 it clearly tell us that Israel will be removed into all the kingdoms of the earth, meaning they are to be spread throughout the 4 corners of the world. The word smitten means grievously or disastrously stricken or afflicted.

> ***Deuteronomy 28:26 And thy carcase shall be meat unto all fowls of the air, and unto the beasts of the earth, and no man shall fray them away.***

> ***Deuteronomy 28:27 The LORD will smite thee with the botch of Egypt, and with the emerods, and with the scab, and with the itch, whereof thou canst not be healed.***

> ***Deuteronomy 28:28 The LORD shall smite thee with madness, and blindness, and astonishment of heart:***

The so called African Americans (Hebrew Israelites/Jews) are in a deep, deep spiritual darkness, they have become ignorant and unaware of the truth about their heritage and their Creator, who is the God of Israel, AHAYAH ASHAR AHAYAH in Hebrew and in English I AM THAT I AM (Exodus 3:14). Instead, they have embraced the slave master's religion, doctrines and culture, not realizing that it was under the auspices of his religion that they were enslaved. The so called Negros state of madness and blindness has caused them to be astonished at our own condition. They are perplexed as to why they seem to be the most hated of all races of men on the face of the earth. They are always the target of discrimination, racism or police brutality. Rodney King, Emit Till, James Byrd Jr. and Ricky Byrdsong, only represent a few of the thousands of victims who have been raped, lynched, beaten, shot and murdered for no apparent reason other than their "racial" identity

> ***Deuteronomy 28:29 And thou shalt grope at noonday, as the blind gropeth in darkness, and thou shalt not prosper in thy ways: and thou shalt be only oppressed and spoiled evermore, and no man shall save thee.***

The above scripture is saying that Israel is going to grope, which means to search around with uncertainty or blindly search. A blind man lives in a world of darkness, and he is forced to grope in order to navigate his surroundings. The scripture also says that no man shall save the children of Israel. The so called Negros has in their history countless men and women who have tried to save this people. Men such as: Frederick Douglass, Nat Turner, Marcus Garvey, Malcolm X, Elijah Muhammad, and a host of others. Freedom will only come through a "spiritual" awakening and healing of the problem that causes our captivity and prolongs our continued oppression. They must come back to the Most High, the God of Israel, and the Creator.

> ***Deuteronomy 28:30 Thou shalt betroth a wife, and another man shall lie with her: thou shalt build an house, and thou shalt not dwell therein: thou shalt plant a vineyard, and shalt not gather the grapes thereof.***

Everything Israel has is going to be taken or belong to someone else. Once again scripture is describing their situation in the West. During slavery, slave owners often took the wives of "Black" (Hebrew Israelites/Jews) slaves and slept with them. This happened during the middle passage, and after the slaves arrived on land.

> ***Deuteronomy 28:31 Thine ox shall be slain before thine eyes, and thou shalt not eat thereof: thine ass shall be violently taken away from before thy face, and shall not be restored to thee: thy sheep shall be given unto thine enemies, and thou shalt have none to rescue them.***

> ***Deuteronomy 28:32 Thy sons and thy daughters shall be given unto another people, and thine eyes shall look, and fail with longing for them all the day long: and there shall be no might in thine hand.***

Black families were ripped apart during the long harsh period of the Atlantic slave trade. In some instances, the sons and daughters of "blacks" were captured while away from their parents, never to see them again. In other cases, entire families were taken into captivity, where parents often watched their children sold to different slave masters and different plantations. In the year 2002 on the local news in Chicago (fox news), they presented a special report called *'The Forgotten Children'*. In this special they were showing how Northern Europeans and some Canadians are adopting black children in Masses. These children were removed from their black parents and given to these other people overseas. The report was shocking, but very informative.

> ***Deuteronomy 28:33 The fruit of thy land, and all thy labors, shall a nation which thou knowest not eat up; and thou shalt be only oppressed and crushed always:***

Because "African Americans" have seen so much discrimination, racism, hatred and death directed toward them, that is has literally driven many of us crazy, to the point that we are filling up the mental institutions in this country. They are also being diagnosed younger, and more often with mental illness than any other racial group in the United States.

> ***Deuteronomy 28:35 The LORD shall smite thee in the knees, and in the legs, with a sore botch that cannot be healed, from the sole of thy foot unto the top of thy head.***
>
> ***Deuteronomy 28:36 The LORD shall bring thee, and thy king which thou shalt set over thee, unto a nation which neither thou nor thy fathers have known; and there shalt thou serve other gods, wood and stone.***

It's not a coincidence that this part of the world was known as the 'NEW WORLD' and this is the land that the Hebrew Israelites ("So called Negros") was brought into as captives, along with their self-appointed kings. They were brought, to a nation neither them nor their fathers knew about. A nation that was not known to the entire world until thousands of years after this prophecy was written. In verse 36 it also says that they are going to worship gods (other religions) of wood and stone. Every religion has a god or gods, so in this verse "gods" also means the various religions. Christianity has Wood Cross and Muslim the Kaaba/Black Stone.

> ***Deuteronomy 28:37 And thou shalt become an astonishment, a proverb, and a byword, among all nations whither the LORD shall lead thee.***

The general attitudes of some "black" people are so disgraceful that it motivates other races to observe them with astonishment. This is the reason many people are always asking the question "why are blacks behind"? "They should be ahead of other groups since they have been here for over 400 years". Proverbs and bywords are nicknames that are used in a scornful manner in substitution for our true nationality. Since the time that the so called Negros have gotten off the slave ships and was brought to America they have been called all types of proverb and bywords. Excuse the language, but here are some bywords: Nigger, Nigga, Monkey, Coon, Porch Money, Gorilla Face, and Dirty.

> ***Deuteronomy 28:38 Thou shalt carry much seed out into the field, and shalt gather but little in; for the locust shall consume it.***
>
> ***Deuteronomy 28:39 Thou shalt plant vineyards, and dress them, but shalt neither drink of the wine, nor gather the grapes; for the worms shall eat them.***
>
> ***Deuteronomy 28:40 Thou shalt have olive trees throughout all thy coasts, but thou shalt not anoint thyself with the oil; for thine olive shall cast his fruit.***
>
> ***Deuteronomy 28:41 Thou shalt beget sons and daughters, but thou shalt not enjoy them; for they shall go into captivity.***

The bible tells us that ancient Israel went into much captivity (Egypt, Assyria, Babylon etc.). But this is exactly how the Hebrew Israelites got here; our fore fathers were brought to this part of the world as captive slaves. Who were captured on the west coast of Africa? This isn't how the Jews (the so called Negreos) or any other ethnic group got here. All other groups came here on their own free will.

> ***Deuteronomy 28:43 The stranger that is within thee shall get up above thee very high; and thou shalt come down very low.***

In this verse 43, stranger refers to other ethnic / racial groups other than the children of Israel. This means that other racial / ethnic groups that live in the same country or city as the Hebrews Israelites will rise up the social / economic ladder higher than the children of Israel, as a collective people.

> ***Deuteronomy 28:44 He shall lend to thee, and thou shalt not lend to him: he shall be the head, and thou shalt be the tail.***

The so called Negros take their money to the stranger (Gentiles), which makes jobs available for their people, while the so called Negros remain unemployed we have the highest unemployment rate in the country despite a "good economy". Only in the Black community do you find every other ethnic group running the businesses, example: The Jewish people own everything the CURRENCY EXCHANGES, BANKS AND LENDING INSTITUTIONS. The Arabs own the GROCERY STORES, & FAST FOOD RESTAURANTS. The Asians own the CLOTHING STORES, NAIL SALONS AND BEAUTY SALONS. The East Indians own the CONVENIENT STORES AND GAS STATIONS. The White Caucasian owns the rest, and Hebrews Israelites own little if any businesses in our community.

> ***Deuteronomy 28:45 Moreover all these curses shall come upon thee, and shall pursue thee, and overtake thee, till thou be destroyed; because thou hearkenedst not unto the voice of the LORD thy God, to keep his commandments and his statutes which he commanded thee:***

> ***Deuteronomy 28:46 And they shall be upon thee for a sign and for a wonder, and upon thy seed for ever.***

No matter where the children of Israel go or what they do these curses are going to be upon them. They are not keeping the Most High laws which he commanded them to do. Israel in the United States has long forgotten the laws of the Most High and this is the sole reason why they have been in terrible conditions since our arrival here. No matter how hard they try, they never get it right. The Most High said the curses are on Israel for a sign. A sign is an Indication; the Most High uses the curses to indicate who his true people are.

> ***Deuteronomy 28:47 Because thou servedst not the LORD thy God with joyfulness, and with gladness of heart, for the abundance of all things;***

Deuteronomy 28:48 Therefore shalt thou serve thine enemies which the LORD shall send against thee, in hunger, and in thirst, and in nakedness, and in want of all things: and he shall put a yoke of iron upon thy neck, until he have destroyed thee

The so called Negros of American oppressors literally put yokes of iron around their necks when they brought us here as captives. A yoke means a shaped piece in a garment, fitted about or below the neck and shoulders or about the hips, from which the rest of the garment hangs. They still have an iron yoke around their necks today. The word yoke also means agency of oppression, subjection, servitude and slavery. Iron is synonymous with power, and strength. Our oppressors have subjected and kept us in a powerful oppression and servitude.

Deuteronomy 28:49 The LORD shall bring a nation against thee from far, from the end of the earth, as swift as the eagle flieth; a nation whose tongue thou shalt not understand;

The far Nation spoken of in prophecy is the western hemisphere, particularly the United States. If you look on any map of the world and look at the so called mid-east, then look at the U.S. not only is the United States far from the mid-east, but it is actually at the end of the earth. Scripture mention this nation is swift as the eagle flieth. It's not a coincidence that the national symbol for the U.S. is the eagle. When the slave traders and catchers came upon the shores of West Africa, the Hebrews didn't understand their languages. The so called Negroes had no knowledge of English or the various other languages the slave traders spoke. In the slave narrative by the slave Olaudah Equiano He tells of his first encounter with European slave traders. This is what he said:

"Their Complexions Too, different so much from ours, their long hair, and the Language they spoke, which was very different from any I had ever heard".

Deuteronomy 28:58 If thou wilt not observe to do all the words of this law that are written in this book, that thou mayest fear this glorious and fearful name, THE LORD THY GOD;

Deuteronomy 28:59 Then the LORD will make thy plagues wonderful, and the plagues of thy seed, even great plagues, and of long continuance, and sore sicknesses, and of long continuance.

These verses are clearly stating that Israel is always going to be a sick and disease stricken people. The so called Negros is only 12% of the U.S. general population, but they have the highest rate of cancer in the U.S. They lead in 8 out of the top 10 cancers. Hebrew Israelites men have the highest rate of prostate cancer in the world, for every 100,000 Hebrew men 185 will get prostate cancer. They are 4x's as likely to get disease as whites and 2x's as likely as Hispanics. They also have the highest rates of HEART DISEASE, DIABETES, HIGH BLOOD PRESSURE, SICKLE CELL ANIMA, STROKES, THYROID TUMORS, ASTHMA, LUPUS, & STD'S (sexually Transmitted Diseases).

Deuteronomy 28:62 And ye shall be left few in number, whereas ye were as the stars of heaven for multitude; because thou wouldest not obey the voice of the LORD thy God.

Deuteronomy 28:63 And it shall come to pass, that as the LORD rejoiced over you to do you good, and to multiply you; so the LORD will rejoice over you to destroy you, and to bring you to nought; and ye shall be plucked from off the land whither thou goest to possess it.

Deuteronomy 28:64 And the LORD shall scatter thee among all people, from the one end of the earth even unto the other; and there thou shalt serve other gods, which

neither thou nor thy fathers have known, even wood and stone.

In verses 64 the true Hebrew Israelites have been scattered from East to West North to South. There probably isn't a country on earth where Hebrew Israelites don't represent some percent of the population. The Hebrews can't be back in the land of Israel as a sovereign nation right now, and at the same time breaking the laws of AHAYAH. This is why the Hebrews Israelites (12 tribes) of the Western Hemisphere are here today in America. In the Countries where Israel is going to be scattered, they are going to serve all kinds of strange gods.

Deuteronomy 28:65 And among these nations shalt thou find no ease, neither shall the sole of thy foot have rest: but the LORD shall give thee there a trembling heart, and failing of eyes, and sorrow of mind:

In verse 65 it states that among those nations where the children of Israel have been scattered we would find no ease or rest for our feet. Here in the Western Hemisphere the Hebrew Israelites have found no ease or peace, but rather horror and terror. Ralph Ginsberg documents some of the terror Hebrew Israelites have suffered in the United States in his book, 100 Years of Lynching.

Deuteronomy 28:66 And thy life shall hang in doubt before thee; and thou shalt fear day and night, and shalt have none assurance of thy life:

What it means is that the so called Negros has feared for their lives since the time of slavery, it is a historical fact that their life has never had any value in this country. This is the reason for centuries, the so called Negros has been murdered and terrorized and no one can seem to stop it. Their lives hang in the balance before them. All the statistics show that they die from violence in the prime of our lives, more than any other ethnic group. In 1990 Hebrew Israelites represented 50% of the 23,760 murder victims known to police. The homicide rate among Hebrew men is generally 6 to 7 times higher than the rate among gentile men. The U.S. Department of Health and Human Services reported that in 1990.

> ***Deuteronomy 28:67 In the morning thou shalt say, Would God it were even! and at even thou shalt say, Would God it were morning! for the fear of thine heart wherewith thou shalt fear, and for the sight of thine eyes which thou shalt see.***

> ***Deuteronomy 28:68 And the LORD shall bring thee into Egypt again with ships, by the way whereof I spake unto thee, Thou shalt see it no more again: and there ye shall be sold unto your enemies for bondmen and bondwomen, and no man shall buy you.***

The so called Negros and the 12 Tribes were brought over here in America (Babylon) on Ships. In Deuteronomy 28:68 it is clear. Once we were over here we were sold and no man would save us. When it says "*And the LORD shall bring thee into Egypt again with ships*" notices the key word again, the word Egypt means bondage. In Exodus 13:3 proves that Egypt means Bondage. America today is spiritual Egypt, in Revelation 11:8 prove that American is spiritual Egypt. When it says "*and there ye shall be sold unto your enemies for bondmen and bondwomen, and no man shall buy you.*" The word bondmen means male slave, the word bondwomen means female slave. Also it says "*no man shall buy you*" what that means is that no man will redeem or save the children of Israel out of their condition that they are in. In a narrative by Friday Jones he explains his account of being sold as a Slave on page 9. In his narrative called Days of Bondage, Being a Brief Narrative of His Trials and Tribulations in Slavery. This is what he said:

> ***"In 1856 my, wife and three children were for sale. I was for sale also. My two oldest children were sold—we were all the property of Dr. Ben Rogers then. Seven other of his servants were for sale, but he refused to sell any of them to a trader, either letting them select homes for themselves or***

> ***he selecting one for them. He was pressed for $10,000—his youngest son got into a difficulty and he had to give a $10,000 bond. He forged $1,000 on the Wilmington N.C., Bank. Jno. O'Neil, of Raleigh, saw my wife and I in Raliegh, and told me to see my master and get him to sell them to him (O'Neil) and it would be a home for them for their life-time. See what a lie a man will tell. A short time after that he sold my wife and youngest child for as much as he gave for the four."***

Since the days that the Most High has brought the children of Israel forefathers out of the land of Egypt even unto this day they have been disobedient to the Father. They have stopped their ears from hearing his voice, and that's why all this evil has come and cleaved unto them as people. They are poor can't get ahead and are in a terrible state as a Nation. They are in America (aka Babylon) and other countries serving other gods and following their own imagination of their wicked hearts. This can be shown in the following scriptures below:

> ***Baruch 1:19-22: Since the day that the Lord brought our forefathers out of the land of Egypt, unto this present day, we have been disobedient unto the Lord our God, and we have been negligent in not hearing his voice.***
>
> ***20 Wherefore the evils cleaved unto us, and the curse, which the Lord appointed by Moses his servant at the time that he brought our fathers out of the land of Egypt, to give us a land that floweth with milk and honey, like as it is to see this day.***
>
> ***21 Nevertheless we have not hearkened unto the voice of the Lord our God, according unto all the words of the prophets, whom he sent unto us:***

22 But every man followed the imagination of his own wicked heart, to serve strange gods, and to do evil in the sight of the Lord our God.—Authorized KJV Apocrypha

Just look at their conditions today. But the Most High said although we have forgotten about him and their special covenant with him. He has not forgotten about us, these curses will be lifted soon and a remnant of Israel shall be saved, I will explain this in the next section.

Enslavement

The children of Israel has been enslaved and sold by the Egyptians, the Muslims and the white Europeans and all the other nations. First let's start with Jacob (Israel) son Joseph. Joseph was already in Egypt and his brothers sold him to the Ishmaelite, because they were jealous of the love that their Father (Jacob) had for him (Genesis 37:3-36). Joseph was also highly favored by the Pharaoh of Egypt. A new Pharaoh arose up and didn't know Joseph nor did he show patronage to the children of Israel. The children of Israel began to multiply rapidly and then a new King over Egypt enslaved the children of Israel and made them serve them with rigor as pointed out in these scriptures below:

Exodus 1:8-14 Now there arose up a new king over Egypt, which knew not Joseph.

9 And he said unto his people, Behold, the people of the children of Israel are more and mightier than we:

10 come on, let us deal wisely with them; lest they multiply, and it come to pass, that, when there falleth out any war, they join also unto our enemies, and fight against us, and so get them up out of the land.

11 Therefore they did set over them taskmasters to afflict them with their burdens. And they built for Pharaoh treasure cities, Pithom and Raamses.

12 But the more they afflicted them, the more they multiplied and grew. And they were grieved because of the children of Israel.

13 And the Egyptians made the children of Israel to serve with rigour:

14 And they made their lives bitter with hard bondage, in morter, and in brick, and in all manner of service in the field: all their service, wherein they made them serve, was with rigour.

Moses, who was a Hebrew, led the Hebrew Israelites out of Egypt in the wilderness (read Exodus chapter 3 to the end of Exodus chapter 14). At this point once the children of Israel were in the wilderness they started to sin against the Most High. The children of Israel were enslaved by the Muslims and the white Europeans also. The European involvement in the slave trade to America lasted over 3 centuries. The Muslim (Arabs) slave trade lasted 14 centuries and still exists in some parts of the world. Two out of three Hebrew Israelites slaves brought to American was men used for agricultural work. Two out of three were women enslaved by the white Europeans and the Muslims for sexual exploitation, concubine, harems, and for military services. Slaves that were transported across the Atlantic about 95% went to Central and South America, Portuguese, French, and Spanish possession. The other 5% went to the United States and that 5% consented of the tribe of Judah who are the so called Negros and the tribe of Gad who are the North American Indians.

During the Trans-Atlantic slave trade Europeans didn't have to venture into the jungles of Africa to capture the Hebrew Israelites because they were already sold into slavery by the African chief or by the Muslim slave traders at the coast. The Trans-Atlantic slave trade had three guilt partners; the African Chiefs, the Muslim Arabs and the white Europeans.

A Remnant of Israel shall be saved

As I previously pointed out, the children of Israel were scattered because of their disobedient to the Most High. They were scattered from Jerusalem and fled into the mountains of Africa during the destruction of Jerusalem in 70 A.D. by the Romans. The Most High never totally destroyed the children of Israel despite their disobedient and being rebellious towards him. That's why the Father promised to save a remnant. Here are some scriptures that prophecies speak about the Most High plan to save a remnant of Israel:

> ***Romans 9:27 Esaias also crieth concerning Israel, Though the number of the children of Israel be as the sand of the sea, a remnant shall be saved:***

Only a remnant of the children of Israel shall be saved and that remnant is those in the latter (end of days) times who will turn to the Father again and serve him in truth and righteousness and those that that the Father put his spirit upon to wake them (children of Israel) up to understand who they really are and who serve him In truth and righteousness will also be a part of that remnant.

> ***Isaiah 6:13 But yet in it shall be a tenth, and it shall return, and shall be eaten: as a teil tree, and as an oak, whose substance is in them, when they cast their leaves: so the holy seed shall be the substance thereof.***

Only a tenth shall return out of Israel/12 Tribes. A small remnant reserved, that number being put indefinitely. This also links back to Zechariah 13:8 where it says that a "*third shall be left therein.*" that is the remnant that will be left out of Israel.

> ***Isaiah 10:20-22 And it shall come to pass in that day, that the remnant of Israel, and such as are escaped of the house of Jacob, shall no more again stay upon him that smote***

them; but shall stay upon the Most High, the Holy One of Israel, in truth.

21 The remnant shall return, even the remnant of Jacob, unto the mighty God.

22 For though thy people Israel be as the sand of the sea, yet a remnant of them shall return: the consumption decreed shall overflow with righteousness.

In Isaiah 11:11 we read that all of the People of Israel (12 Tribes) will be gathered from the above places mentioned in scripture. This is a future prophecy. The prophet Ezekiel also identifies this remnant of Israel:

Ezekiel 37:11-12 Then he said unto me, Son of man, these bones are the whole house of Israel: behold, they say, Our bones are dried, and our hope is lost: we are cut off for our parts.

12 Therefore prophesy and say unto them, Thus saith the Lord GOD; Behold, O my people, I will open your graves, and cause you to come up out of your graves, and bring you into the land of Israel.

Ezekiel 37:21-24 And say unto them, Thus saith the Lord GOD; Behold, I will take the children of Israel from among the heathen, whither they be gone, and will gather them on every side, and bring them into their own land:

22 And I will make them one nation in the land upon the mountains of Israel; and one king shall be king to them all: and they shall be no more two nations, neither shall they be divided into two kingdoms any more at all:

1 Neither shall they defile themselves any more with their idols, nor with their detestable things, nor with

any of their transgressions: but I will save them out of all their dwelling places, wherein they have sinned, and will cleanse them: so shall they be my people, and I will be their God.

2 And David my servant shall be king over them; and they all shall have one shepherd: they shall also walk in my judgments, and observe my statutes, and do them.

The 37th chapter of Ezekiel is speaking about the children of Israel who were driven away from their homelands. Yet the Most High did not completely destroy them.

★ 18 ★

Religion

Much confusion exists regarding different religious beliefs. My research and through biblical facts has lead me to come to these conclusion about these religions. In this chapter I will be covering Christianity, Jehovah Witness and Muslims. Many of the children of Israel are stuck in these religions and they are serving other gods as prophecy has already foretold us. My intent and wishes are not to offend anyone, but to shed light about these religions to name a few on how they keep the Most High people from truly serving him. All the prophets in the Bible taught that there was one God, and that is the God of Israel (AHAYAH AHSER AHAYAH—I AM THAT I AM). So if the Most High prophets taught that it is one true God, and then we must ask this question, why is it so many different religions? That's why the first Commandment is very important, and it is read like this:

Exodus 20:3 Thou shalt have no other Gods before me.

The Most High God tells us to not have any other gods before him. What we must understand is that there is only one true God as I have already stated (Psalm 96:4-5). When we are in these religions it is important to know that each religion have their own gods (idols). Majority of Christians will tell you that Christianity is a religion that is derived from Jesus (Yashaya); one must ask the question is that true? The answer to that is No. The Bible identifies the Messiah as a Jew (Tribe of Judah) (John 4:9-10). Jesus (Yashaya) kept the laws of the Most High like: the Passover, the Sabbath, the Dietary Law and other Holy days. In Christianity they teach and tell the people that they don't have to keep the laws of the Most High and that the laws are done away with. We must keep the laws of the Most High, as it is written in:

> ***Matthew 15:17-18 Think not that I am come to destroy the law, or the prophets: I am not come to destroy, but to fulfil.***
>
> ***18 For verily I say unto you, Till heaven and earth pass, one jot or one tittle shall in no wise pass from the law, till all be fulfilled.***
>
> ***Baruch 4:1 This is the book of the commandments of the Most High, and the law that endureth for ever: all they that keep it shall come to life; but such as leave it shall die.*** *- Authorized KJV Apocrypha*

Why do they say that Christianity comes from Jesus (Yashaya) and majority of Christians don't even keep the laws of the Most High? Especially the children of Israel (12 Tribes). I would also like to point out that the word Christ was never apart of Jesus name. Christ means 'anointed one' it is pronounced in the Greek as 'Christos' since the New Testament was written in Greek as I pointed out previously in the book. So now we can see why the Roman Catholic Church would add that to the name to further deceive you to believe this is his name when it's not.

I would like to start off by saying Christianity is not the truth. It's full of Lies and Deception. This is the world's largest religion and it has deceived our people far too long. We need to understand that everything you see and hear is not always true. I just pray and hope that you really get the message that I am trying to convey to you. I repeat Christianity is full of lies and deception. They teach that the creator or the God of Israel doesn't have a name and his name is God. The Father gave us his name. This can be pointed out in Exodus chapter 3 when Moses asks the Most High what he shall tell the children of Israel his name was:

> ***Exodus 3:13-15 And Moses said unto God, Behold, when I come unto the children of Israel, and shall say unto them, The God of your fathers hath sent me unto you; and they shall say to me, What is his name? what shall I say unto them?***
>
> ***14 And God said unto Moses, I AM THAT I AM: and he said, Thus shalt thou say unto the children of Israel, I AM hath sent me unto you.***
>
> ***15 And God said moreover unto Moses, Thus shalt thou say unto the children of Israel, The LORD God of your fathers, the God of Abraham, the God of Isaac, and the God of Jacob, hath sent me unto you: this is my name for ever, and this is my memorial unto all generations.***

Moses asks the Most High, what shall he say to the children of Israel when he goes to the children of Israel and say "*The God of your fathers hath sent me unto you*" and the Most High said "***I AM THAT I AM***: and he said, "*Thus shalt thou say unto the children of Israel,* **I AM** *hath sent me unto you.*" The Father's true name in Hebrew is **AHAYAH ASHAR AHAYAH** *(***AHAYAH—I AM***)*. Notice in verse 15 he said "*this is my name forever*," So if this is the Father's true name one must ask the question to why don't Christianity call upon the Creator or the Most High true name. We see that God is not his name; in fact the word God is pagan and can also mean an idol. The Old Testament was written in Hebrew and the New Testament in Greek. Also you can find the father true name in the JPS Hebrew-English Tanakh. Remember Hebrew is read from right to left and in the Ancient Hebrew there are no e soundings.

I would also like to point out that in Christianity they call upon the Son (the Messiah) Name as "Jesus". That is a roman Greek god named Iēsous. The Messiah's real name in Hebrew is Yashaya which mean in the Hebrew salvation, saving. What we must understand is that we know from the previous chapter that the Messiah was a Hebrew Israelites. The letter J is the newest letter in the English alphabet. Also there is no J sound in the Ancient Hebrew language let along the letter J. So if the letter J is the newest letter in the alphabet and the Messiah was a Jew from the tribe of Judah (Hebrews 7:14) then his name can't be Jesus (Iesous) that is a Greek name and they (Roman Catholic Church) put it into English form, it's not a Hebrew name. I would like to prove my case with this scripture:

> ***Acts 26:14 And when we were all fallen to the earth, I heard a voice speaking unto me, and saying in the Hebrew tongue, Saul, Saul, why persecutest thou me? it is hard for thee to kick against the pricks.***

In Acts 26:14 we read that Paul heard Jesus (Yashaya) speak to him in the Hebrew tongue. The messiah was a Black Jew from the tribe of Judah as stated in Hebrews 7:14 as I pointed out previously. This means that if the Messiah spoke Hebrew and was from the Tribe of Judah then his name must be Hebrew as well. The Messiah true name is YASHAYA in the Ancient Hebrew tongue as I pointed out. Yashaya means salvation, saving, safety, liberty, and deliverance.

Many so called Christians and as well as others think that Jesus (Yashaya) died on an actual cross. Long before the Christian era, crosses were used by the ancient Babylonians as symbols in their worship of the fertility god Tammuz. The indisputable sign of Tammuz, the mystic Tau of the Babylonians and Egyptians, was brought into the Church chiefly because of Constantine. We know through the divine scriptures that the messiah was hanged on a Tree because he was a Hebrew Israelites from the tribe of Judah, because the children of Israel were told to hang a man on a tree if he has committed a sin worthy of death. This is shown in this scripture below:

Deuteronomy 21:22-23 And if a man committed a sin worthy of death, and he be to be put to death, and thou hang him on a tree:

23 His body shall not remain all night upon the tree, but thou shalt in any wise bury him that day; (for he that is hanged is accursed of God) that thy land be not defiled, which the Lord thy God giveth thee for an inheritance.

In verse 22 it is clear to us that if a man committed a sin worthy of death, then he is to be hanged on a tree. Here are more scriptures to prove that he was hanged on a tree:

Acts 5:30 The God our fathers raised up Jesus, whom ye slew and hangd on a tree.

1 Peter 2:24 Who his own self bare our sins in his own body on the tree, that we, being dead to sins, should live unto righteousness: by whose stripes ye were healed

Acts 13:29 And when they had fulfilled all that was written on him, they took him down from the tree, and laid him in a sepulchre.

It clearly points out that the Messiah was hanged on a tree. Peter clearly says that Jesus (Yashaya) bare our sins in his own body on a Tree. It is also clear that once Jesus (Yashaya) had passed over (died) they took his body from the tree a placed it in a tomb. Also another thing that I would like to point out is that most of the so called Negros and other 12 Tribes are unaware why they go to church (Congregation/ Assembly) on Sunday which is the first day of the week; I will further go into more detail within this chapter. I must also point out that the Roman Catholic Church inserted the word Church into the KJV Bible. In place of the word church it was supposed to say, congregation or Assembly. They also inserted the word virgin to mean that someone hadn't had sexual intercourse, in place of the original meaning of the word virgin which is supposed to be a young maid or maiden. What we must understand is that the so called Negroes never had a Religion and Christianity was forced upon the slaves when they got off slave ships and onto the plantation. The slaves were forced to go to church and thus becoming brainwashed and ripped from their heritage.

There has been a strong delusion within the church (Congregation) about the Rapture Doctrine. Many so called Christians believe in this false doctrine and don't fully understand who is behind it. My research has lead me to uncover those who had a part in spreading this false doctrine to deceive the masses. I will go into a little history as to who is behind the Rapture doctrine. The "Rapture" teaching was not taught by the early Church, it was not taught by Church of the first centuries, it was not taught by the Reformers, it was not taught by anyone (except a couple of Roman Catholic theologians) until about the year 1830. At the time of the Reformation, the early Protestants widely held and were convinced the Pope was the supreme individual embodiment and personification of the spirit of antichrist, and the Roman Church, the Harlot System of Revelation seventeen. This understanding was responsible for bringing millions of believers out of the Roman Catholic religious system. John Nelson Darby is responsible for the spreading and teaching of the Rapture doctrine, along with his other Plymouth Brethren. Edward Irving (1792-1834), a Scottish Presbyterian and forerunner of the Pentecostal and Charismatic movements, translated Lacunza's work from Spanish into English in a book titled *The Coming of Messiah in Glory and Majesty with a Preliminary Discourse*, published in London in 1827 by L.B. Seeley & Sons. His church in London seated one thousand people and was packed week after week with a congregation drawn from the most brilliant and influential circles of society. Irving discovered Lacunza's book and was deeply shaken by it. At this time Irving heard what he believed to be a voice from heaven commanding him to preach the *Secret Rapture of the Saints.* Irving then began to hold Bible conferences throughout Scotland, Emphasizing the coming of the Messiah to rapture His Church. About this same time there began the emergence of a new movement which came to be known as the *Plymouth Brethren.* A man by the name of John Nelson Darby was the leading spirit among the Plymouth Brethren from 1830 onward. Darby was from a prosperous Irish family, was educated as a lawyer, took high honors at Dublin University, and then turned aside, to his father's chagrin, to become a minister. John Nelson Darby (1800-1882), Irving and Darby were contemporaries, though associated with different spiritual movements. Another series of meetings were in progress at this time. A Church of Ireland clergyman, later with the Plymouth Brethren, also promoted Futurism and a secret rapture. Darby's biographers refer to him as *"the father of dispensationalism."* And the crown jewel in the kingdom of dispensationalism is, of course, the so-called *SECRET RAPTURE!* Darby, called the 'father of dispensationalism', was responsible for the widespread dissemination of the new and novel pretribulation doctrine beginning around 1830 through his ministry in the Plymouth Brethren movement. The doctrine soon spread to America and was widely popularized by the Scofield Reference Bible. The rapture doctrine, it began as a Roman Catholic invention. The Jesuit priest *Ribera's* writings influenced the Jesuit priest *Lacunza,* Lacunza influenced *Irving,* Irving influenced *Darby,* Darby influenced *Scofield,* Scofield and Darby influenced *D. L. Moody,* and Moody influenced *the Pentecostal Movement.*

It is also important to point out that allot of the Most High chosen people (Hebrew Israelites/Jews) are part of a false religion called Jehovah witness. I must also point out that this religion is based on mind control just like that others are. In fact the Founder of this occult organization was a 33rd Degree Free Mason. The founder of this religion is Pastor Charles Taze Russell. He was also a 33rd Degree Mason. He also believed it was appropriate to lie to opposers. He didn't see anything wrong with being a Mason while at the same time a so call Christian. He also co-published The Herald of the Morning magazine, with its founder, N. H. Barbour. This magazine was to so call foretells the coming of Christ in 1874. Russell is part of the Russell bloodline of the Illuminate, which also founded the infamous Skull and Bones Society. My desires are not to talk about the founder or slander his name, but to shed light to the readers about this false mean spirited religion. Charles T. Russell, the founder of the Jehovah's Witnesses, would indicate that he had ties with the Masons. He used Masonic symbols. The Watchtower drawing that graced early publications right up to a couple of Decades ago was pure Masonic. Other Masonic symbols were used frequently on his publications.

Russell also believed in the Masonic belief of a "New World Order". Russell believed in Masonry until his death, as evidence by the Masonic gravestone that he lies beneath. He also told his followers to read the book, Angels and Women". This was a book dictated about a "fallen Angels" (demon) to a women spirit medium. Those who are a part of this false and evil religion I would advise you to do more research before you just start to follow a man made up religion. In a speech that Pastor Russell gave at a Special 1913 Convention Report of the International Bible Students. Under the subject of "The Temple of God" is a discourse by Pastor Russell reported verbatim on pages 120 these words:

> ***"I am very glad to have this particular opportunity of saying a word about some of the things in which we agree with our Masonic friends, because we are speaking in a building dedicated to Masonry and we also are Mason. I am a free a accepted Mason, If I may carry the matter to its full length, because that is what our Masonic brethren like to tell us, that they are free and accepted Mason. That is there style of putting it. Now I am a free an accepted Mason. I trust we all are, but not after the style of our Masonic Brethren. We have no qaurall with them. I am not going to say a word against Masons, and I can appreciate that there are certain very precious truths that are held in part by our Masonic friends. I have talked to them at times, and they have said, How do you know about all of these things? We thought nobody knew about all of these things expect those who had access to our very highest logic"***

The Founder(s) of this false religion even built a mansion for the Prophets in the Bible. They thought all the prophets in the bible were coming back soon in 1878. The mansion was called the, Beth Sarim that they built. The ungodly has mixed the Gospel of truth and Masonry. The most deceptive teachings are those that have mixed truth with error. I can only pray that this information will find its way too many modern day Jehovah's Witnesses who revere this false prophet and his twisted teachings. I pray many eyes will be opened and modern so called Jehovah's Witnesses will begin an investigation into their roots. The Most High chosen people especially needs to come out of this false religion. There are many of the children of Israel who is a part of a false Religion known today as being a Muslim. As I pointed out in the book previously under the section called "Enslavement" that the Muslims bought and sold the children of Israel. How is it that the so called Negros (Tribe of Judah /Jews) and the rest of the 12 Tribes follow a religion that was never meant for them and founded by Arabs? They follow these so called man made up religions is due to them being lost and not knowing who they are (Jeremiah 17:4), but really religion confuses the people even more. Although Islam is today a monotheist religion, its roots are in paganism. Islam is a religious system that begun in the 7th century by Muhammad. Muslims follow the teachings of the Qur'an and strive to keep the Five Pillars. Muhammad had many male and female slaves. He used to buy and sell them, but he purchased more. "Al-ilah" was later shortened to Allah before Muhammad began promoting his new religion in 610 AD.

Allah is the Arabic word for "God" used by Muslims. I would like to address that Islam worship the Moon. Moon worship has been practiced in Arabia since 2000 BC. The crescent moon is the most common symbol of this pagan moon worship as far back as 2000 BC. In Mecca, there was a god named Hubal who was Lord of the Kabah. There is evidence that Hubal was referred to as "Allah". If you look on many of the temples you will see a moon crescent symbol and the Nation of Islam religious symbol is a crescent moon. The children of Israel have defiled themselves with this religion and many others. This is prophecies that they would go and worship the other gods and the hosts of heaven:

Deuteronomy 17:3 And hath gone and served other gods, and worshipped them, either the sun, or moon, or any of the host of heaven, which I have not commanded;

Jeremiah 8:2 And they shall spread them before the sun, and the moon, and all the host of heaven, whom they have loved, and whom they have served, and after whom they have walked, and whom they have sought, and whom they have worshipped: they shall not be gathered, nor be buried; they shall be for dung upon the face of the earth.

These two scriptures above lets us know that the children of Israel would go and serve other gods. In Islam they worship a black Stone, called the black Stone of Mecca or the Kaaba stone, it's a Muslim relic. It is the eastern cornerstone of the Kaaba, the ancient sacred stone building towards which Muslims pray, in the center of the Grand Mosque in Mecca, Saudi Arabia. The pilgrims circle the Kaaba as part of the Tawaf ritual of the Hajj, many of them try, and if possible, to stop and kiss the Black Stone, emulating the kiss that it received from the Islamic prophet Muhammad. The Black Stone of Kaaba or Mecca in Arabic is called Al-hajar Al-aswad. The word Kaaba—Ka'ba—Ka'bah means Cube. This is also mentioned in the Holy Scripture that the children of Isarel would go and serve other gods, and a stone is one of them:

Deuteronomy 29:17 And ye have seen their abominations, and their idols, wood and stone, silver and gold, which were among them :)

It is clear that the Nation of Islam (Muslims) worship a Stone, The Kaaba is nothing more but a stone, the children of Israel was warned, but they worshiped it anyway. They (Muslims) believe that this stone fell from the sky during the time of Adam and Eve, and that it has the power to cleanse worshippers of their sins by absorbing them into itself. They say that the Black Stone was once a pure and dazzling white and it has turned black because of the sins it has absorbed over the years. I would also like to point out that it is remarkable, however, that even though the temple contained 360 idols worshipped before Muhammad's Prophet Hood, the black stone was never kissed or made an idol of worship. In fact, the Ka'ba was never worshipped by the idolaters prior to Muhammad's Prophet Hood. The building contained idols of worship but the building itself was never an object of worship.

The Understanding Of John 3:16

It is very important to point out that Majority of Christianity like to quote John 3:16 and don't understand what's really being said. Religious intuitions teach that the Most high, the God of Israel loves everybody, this is true to those who serve him in truth and righteousness and reverence his people who are the children of Israel (12 Tribes). Salvation is to the Jews, what that means is that all nations must come to the true Jews to receive salvation (Acts 13:47), because the Most High only gave Israel his words (Romans 3:1-4). I will further discuss the duty of the Most High people later in the book. I will provide a full breakdown of what John 3:16 really means:

> ***John 3:16 For God so loved the world, that he gave his only begotten Son, that whosoever believeth in him should not perish, but have everlasting life.***

For the Most High so love the world, this seems like it is talking about the whole world and all the Nations. The word world means 'A particular class of people, with common interests, aims, etc.'

> ***John 17:9 I pray for them: I pray not for the world, but for them which thou hast given me; for they are thine.***

The Messiah says that he *"pray for them and not the world"*. The Messiah said he pray not for the world. The them are the Hebrew Israelites/Jews in which he was sent to redeem them for their sins.

> ***John 6:37-39 All that the Father giveth me shall come to me; and him that cometh to me I will in no wise cast out.***

> ***For I came down from heaven, not to do mine own will, but the will of him that sent me.***
>
> ***And this is the Father's will which hath sent me, that of all which he hath given me I should lose nothing, but should raise it up again at the last day.***

In John 6:39 it says "that of all which he hath given me" meaning there is a different between everybody in the Earth and a group of people that the Most High gave to the Messiah and that group of people is the Children of Israel. Then it goes on and gives us a clue to who those people are, when it says "but should raise it up again". That word again is very important, because of that people who the Father gave the Messiah his Son he will raise them (Hebrew Israelites) up again in the last days. In order to be raised up again you had to be up at one point before then taken down. You can't be raised up again if you were never up in the first place. Let's continue to read for more understanding.

> ***Deuteronomy 7:6 For thou art an holy people unto the Lord thy God: the Lord thy God hath chosen thee to be a special people unto himself, above all people that are upon the face of the earth.***

This is Moses speaking to the Children of Israel. It says "above all people that are upon the face of the earth". The word above mean, up. So we see that the children of Israel were set up above all the people upon the face of the earth by the Most High, because the Most High chose them to give his laws to. The Nation of Israel received these blessing, but later on fell as a nation due their disobedient.

> ***Acts 1:6 When they therefore were come together, they asked of him, saying, Lord, wilt thou at this time restore again the kingdom to Israel?***

The disciples ask the Messiah this question "Lord, wilt thou at this time restore again the kingdom to Israel?" Israel was the Nation that was up but fell and that needed to be restored again, that's why the Messiah said in John 17:9 "*I pray for them: I pray not for the world,*" And in John 6:39 he said "*but should raise it up again at the last day*", meaning raise the Nation of Israel back up again. We know that John 3:16 isn't talking about everybody in the World, it's talking about a group of people. Look at the Definition for the word world. The word world means 'A particular class of people, with common interests, aims, etc. Since we know that the word world also means a Particular class of people, with common interests, and aims. We can now understand why the Messiah said in John 17:9 "I pray for them: I pray not for the world, the them is the Nation of Israel". Also the words restore means 'To bring back into existence, use, or the like; reestablish'.

Acts 5:30-31 The God of our fathers raised up Jesus, whom ye slew and hanged on a tree.

31 Him hath the God exalted with his right hand to be a Prince and a Saviour, for to give repentance to Israel, and forgiveness of sins.

According to verse 31 the Messiah came to take away the sins of Israel. Please read the Precepts to Matthew 1:21, Ephesians 1:17, and Colossians 1:14, to see that he came to take away the sins of Israel. The whole conclusion of John 3:16 when it says "*For the Most High so loved the world*" this cant mean everybody its talking about a specific group of people. That's why the Messiah said this:

Matthew 15:24 But he answered and said, I am not sent but unto the lost sheep of the house of Israel.

That specific group of people is the Children of Israel.

The Change Of The Sabbath

It's very important to know the true day of the Sabbath. In Christianity they teach that the Sunday is the Sabbath when in fact it's Saturday. The Romans themselves admired the religion and culture of Greece. They adopted Greek gods and blended them into their own religions. The result was a mixture of ancestor worship, emperor worship, and sun worship, a religion that included not one god, but many. The Jews, on the other hand, worshipped only one God, the God of Israel (AHAYAH). Though surrounded by the images of Greek and Roman deities, they served other gods and it lead to them rebelling against the God of Israel as I mentioned earlier in the book.

In the Old Testament, the Most High established the Sabbath as the celebration of His creative work and as a day of freedom from labor and it was a sign between the children of Israel. On the Sabbath there is no work to be done, sex, buying, and etc. It's a Holy day a day of rest. See scripture below:

> ***Genesis 2:2-3 And on the seventh day the God ended his work which he had made; and he rested on the seventh day from all his work which he had made.***
>
> ***3 And God blessed the seventh day, and sanctified it: because that in it he had rested from all his work which God created and made.***

Christianity was not the only religion that was gaining popularity within the Roman Empire. Various forms of sun worship were also attracting adherents, among who were the emperors themselves. There had been other forms of sun worship that were also in vogue. When Nero commissioned a gigantic statue in his own honor, it featured a likeness of the emperor's head in sun-god fashion. Known as the Colossus of Nero, it stood 37 meters high. Future emperors would alter the features dedicate it to the "unconquerable sun." Aurelian, emperor from 270-275 AD, established a state religion that included worship of the emperor and the sun. Constantine was, like Aurelian, a worshiper of the sun. He was also the first Emperor to profess belief in Christianity, and shall I say the founder also of this false religion. Constantine's personal religion was a mixture of Mithraic sun worship and Christianity. According to his Christian biographer, Eusebius, he taught all his armies to zealously honor the Lord's Day—Sunday—referring to it as "the day of light and of the sun." This was distinctly pagan terminology.

The Roman Catholic Church changed the Original Sabbath of the Bible to Sunday in 321 (A.D.). Emperor Constantine on March 7, 325 (A. D.) issued the first civil legislation proclaiming Sunday, the venerable day of the Sun, a day of rest. What we must understand is that this is prophecy that the Roman Catholic Church would change the Sabbath day (Day 7) to Sunday (Day 1), due to them worshipping the Sun. Here is the scripture to prove this:

> ***Daniel 7:25 And he shall speak great words against the most High, and shall wear out the saints of the most High, and think to change times and laws: and they shall be given into his hand until a time and times and the dividing of time.***

The is part of the Ten Commandments, the Sabbath is to be remembered and kept as a Holy day:

> ***Exodus 20:8 Remember the sabbath day, to keep it holy.***
>
> ***Exodus 31:12-17 And Lord spake unto Moses, saying, Speak thou also unto the children of Israel, saying, Verily my sabbaths ye shall keep: for it is a sign between me and you throughout your generations; that ye may know that I am the Lord that doth sanctify you.***
>
> ***Ye shall keep the sabbath therefore; for it is holy unto you: every one that defileth it shall surely be put to death: for whosoever doeth any work therein, that soul shall be cut off from among his people.***
>
> ***Six days may work be done; but in the seventh is the sabbath of rest, holy to the Lord: whosoever doeth any work in the sabbath day, he shall surely be put to death.***

Wherefore the children of Israel shall keep the sabbath, to observe the sabbath throughout their generations, for a perpetual covenant.

It is a sign between me and the children of Israel for ever: for in six days the LORD made heaven and earth, and on the seventh day he rested, and was refreshed.

This is a sign between the children of Israel (Jews/12 Tribes of Israel).

Roman Catholic Confessions

People have been heavily deceived when it comes to worshipping the Most High God. They worship him on Sunday which is the first day and not Saturday (Sabbath) which is the last day of the week. Most Churches are about money and not teaching the true Laws, Statues and commandments of the Most High God. The Roman Catholic Church changed the Sabbath to Sunday to worship the Sun. Here are some confessions about the Roman Catholic Church admitting to the change of the Sabbath to Sunday from various sources.

This is the actual Letter of Catholic Church
Admitting Changing the Sabbath to Sunday

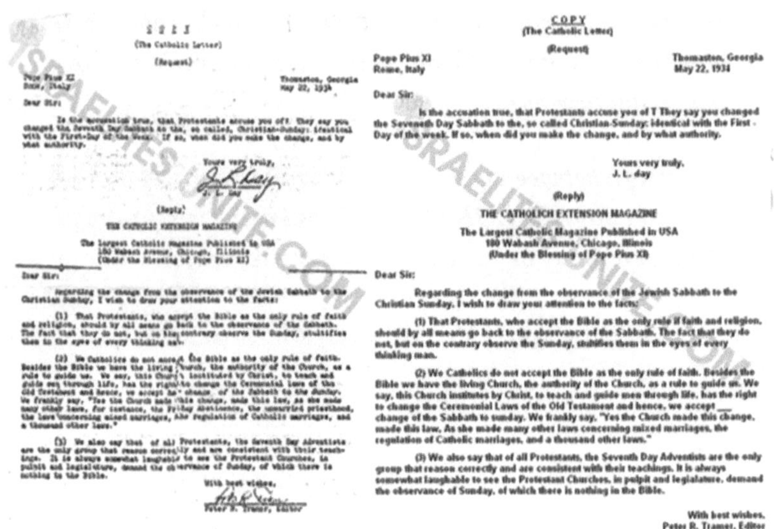

COPY
(The Catholic Letter)

(Request)

Pope Pius XI
Rome, Italy

Thomaston, Georgia
May 22, 1934

Dear Sir:

Is the accuation true, that Protestants accuse you of T They say you changed the Seveneth Day Sabbath to the, so called Christian-Sunday: identical with the First - Day of the week. If so, when did you make the change, and by what authority.

Yours very truly,
J. L. day

(Reply)

THE CATHOLICH EXTENSION MAGAZINE

The Largest Catholic Magazine Published in USA
180 Wabash Avenue, Chicago, Illinois
(Under the Blessing of Pope Pius XI)

Dear Sir:

Regarding the change from the observance of the Jewish Sabbath to the Christian Sunday, I wish to draw your attention to the facts:

(1) That Protestants, who accept the Bible as the only rule if faith and religion, should by all means go back to the observance of the Sabbath. The fact that they do not, but on the contrary observe the Sunday, stultifies them in the eyes of every thinking man.

(2) We Catholics do not accept the Bible as the only rule of faith. Besides the Bible we have the living Church, the authority of the Church, as a rule to guide us. We say, this Church institutes by Christ, to teach and guide men through life, has the right to change the Ceremonial Laws of the Old Testament and hence, we accept ___ change of the Sabbath to sunday. We frankly say, "Yes the Church made this change, made this law, As she made many other laws concerning mixed marriages, the regulation of Catholic marriages, and a thousand other laws."

(3) We also say that of all Protestants, the Seventh Day Adventists are the only group that reason correctly and are consistent with their teachings. It is always somewhat laughable to see the Protestant Churches, in pulpit and legislature, demand the observance of Sunday, of which there is nothing in the Bible.

With best wishes,
Peter R. Tramer, Editor

"Sunday, the first day of the week, is heralded today as the "Christian Sabbath". But it has not always been so! Since ancient times, Sunday has been a day in which pagans, witches, shamans, and other occult and spiritualistic peoples worshipped the sun, hence the name--Sun-day. It was not a day to worship the God of heaven, but to worship the god of this earth--Lucifer or Satan or the devil, and can be traced all the way back to ancient Babylon and Nimrod. As the first day of the week is almost universally observed by Christians today instead of the seventh day Sabbath of creation which the Creator required that we must remember to keep holy (see Genesis 2:2-3; Exodus 20:8-11), the question needs to be asked: When was this change made? The Roman Catholic Church states: "Perhaps the boldest thing, the most revolutionary change the Church ever did, happened in the first century. The holy day, the Sabbath, was changed from Saturday to Sunday. 'The day of the Lord' was chosen, not from any direction noted in the Scriptures, but from the Church's sense of its own power. People who think that the Scriptures should be the sole authority, should logically. Keep Saturday holy." **St. Catherine Church Sentinel, Algonac, Michigan, May 21, 1995**.

"For example, nowhere in the Bible do we find that Christ or the Apostles ordered that the Sabbath be changed from Saturday to

Sunday. We have the commandment of God given to Moses to keep holy the Sabbath day, that is the 7th day of the week, Saturday. Today most Christians keep Sunday because it has been revealed to us by the Roman Catholic Church outside the Bible." **Catholic Virginian, October 3, 1947, p. 9, article "To Tell You the Truth**."

"Is not every Christian obliged to sanctify Sunday and to abstain on that day from unnecessary servile work? Is not the observance of this law among the most prominent of our sacred duties? But you may read the Bible from Genesis to Revelation, and you will not find a single line authorizing the sanctification of Sunday. The Scriptures enforce the religious observance of Saturday, a day which we never sanctify." **James Cardinal Gibbons, The Faith of Our Fathers (1917 edition), p. 72-73 (16th Edition, p 111; 88th Edition, p. 89).**

"Written by the finger of God on two tables of stone, this Divine code (ten commandments) was received from the Almighty by Moses amid the thunders of Mount Sinai...Christ resumed these Commandments in the double precept of charity--love of God and of the neighbour; He proclaimed them as binding under the New Law in Matthew 19 and in the Sermon on the Mount (Matthew 5)....The (Catholic) Church, on the other hand, after changing the day of rest from the Jewish Sabbath, or seventh day of the week, to the first, made the Third Commandment refer to Sunday as the day to be kept holy as the Lord's Day....He (God) claims one day out of the seven as a memorial to Himself, and this must be kept holy." **The Catholic Encyclopedia, vol. 4, "The Ten Commandments", 1908 edition by Robert Appleton Company; and 1999 On-line edition by Kevin Knight, Imprimatur, John M. Farley, Archbishop of New York**.

"The Catholic church for over one thousand years before the existence of a Protestant, by virtue of her divine mission, changed the day from Saturday to Sunday. The Protestant World at its birth found the Christian Sabbath too strongly entrenched to run counter to its existence; it was therefore placed under the necessity of acquiescing in the arrangement, thus implying the (Catholic) Church's right to change the day, for over three hundred years. The christian Sabbath is therefore to this day, the

acknowledged offspring of the Catholic Church as spouse of the Holy Ghost, without a word of remonstrance from the Protestant World." **James Cardinal Gibbons in the Catholic Mirror, September 23, 1983.**

"They (the Protestants) deem it their duty to keep the Sunday holy. Why? Because the Catholic Church tells them to do so. They have no other reason....The observance of Sunday thus comes to be an ecclesiastical law entirely distinct from the divine law of Sabbath observance....The author of the Sunday law...is the Catholic Church." **Ecclesiastical Review, February, 1914.**

"The Sunday...is purely a creation of the Catholic Church." **American Catholic Quarterly Review, January, 1883.**

"Sunday...is the law of the Catholic Church alone." **American Sentinel *(Catholic)***, June, 1893.

"Sunday is a Catholic institution and its claim to observance can be defended only on Catholic principles....From beginning to end of Scripture there is not a single passage that warrants the transfer of weekly public worship from the last day of the week to the first." **Catholic Press, Sydney, Australia, August, 1900.**

"It is well to remind the Presbyterians, Baptists, Methodists, and all other Christians, that the Bible does not support them anywhere in their observance of Sunday. Sunday is an institution of the Roman Catholic Church, and those who observe the day observe a commandment of the Catholic Church." **Priest Brady, in an address reported in *The News*, Elizabeth, New Jersey, March 18, 1903.**

"The authority of the church could therefore not be bound to the authority of the Scriptures, because the Church had changed... the Sabbath into Sunday, not by command of Christ, but by its own authority." ***Canon and Tradition*, p. 263.**

"From this we may understand how great is the authority of the church in interpreting or explaining to us the commandments of

God – an authority which is acknowledged by the universal practice of the whole Christian world, even of those sects which profess to take the holy Scriptures as their sole rule of faith, since they observe as the day of rest not the seventh day of the week demanded by the Bible, but the first day. Which we know is to be kept holy, only from the tradition and teaching of the Catholic church." **Henry Gibson,** *Catechism Made Easy*, **# 2, 9th edition, vol. 1, p. 341-342**.

★ 19 ★

The Most High Chosen People

As I have pointed out before the Hebrew Israelites are the Most High chosen people. They were chosen to teach the word of the Most High. They are sent to be a light to the Gentiles; I will speak more about this in the next chapter. The Most High chosen people are a Holy people, so holy that they were set apart from the other Nations. They were given Laws, Statutes, and commandments. I will give a breakdown down through scripture to show how holy the children of Israel are:

> ***Deuteronomy 4:7-8 For what nation is there so great, who hath God so nigh unto them, as the Lord our God is in all things that we call upon him for?***
>
> ***8 And what nation is there so great, that hath statutes and judgments so righteous as all this law, which I set before you this day?***

Moses asked the children of Israel 2 question he said "For what nation is there so great and what nation is there so great, that hath statutes and judgments as righteous as all this law". They are as holy as a people that as a Nation we are the only people that have Statutes laws and judgments.

> ***Deuteronomy 7:6-8 For thou art an holy people unto the Lord H thy God: the Lord thy God hath chosen thee to be a special people unto himself, above all people that are upon the face of the earth.***
>
> ***The Lord did not set his love upon you, nor choose you, because ye were more in number than any people; for ye were the fewest of all people:***
>
> ***But because the Lord loved you, and because he would keep the oath which he had sworn unto your fathers, hath the Lord brought you out with a mighty hand, and redeemed you out of the house of bondmen, from the hand of Pharaoh king of Egypt.***

The children of Israel are a special people and above all the people (Gentiles) upon the face of the earth. In verse 8 it said that the Most High loved them, the 12 Tribes of Israel and delivered our forefathers out of the hand of the Egyptians.

> ***Matthew 5:13-14 Ye are the salt of the earth: but if the salt have lost his savour, wherewith shall it be salted? it is thenceforth good for nothing, but to be cast out, and to be trodden under foot of men.***
>
> ***14 Ye are the light of the world. A city that is set on an hill cannot be hid.***

The children of Israel (Hebrew Israelites) are the salt of the world, the so called Negros and the rest of the 12 Tribes. They are the ones that give the world flavor. The children of Israel are great at anything they do, like playing sports, and entertainment. The Hebrew Israelites (children of Israel) are the best at what they do, that's why it says they are the salt of the world.

> ***Leviticus 20:24-26 But I have said unto you, Ye shall inherit their land, and I will give it unto you to possess it, a land that floweth with milk and honey: I am the Most High your power, which have separated you from other people.***
>
> ***Ye shall therefore put difference between clean beasts and unclean, and between unclean fowls and clean: and ye shall not make your souls abominable by beast, or by fowl, or by any manner of living thing that creepeth on the ground, which I have separated from you as unclean.***
>
> ***And ye shall be holy unto me: for I the Most High am holy, and have severed you from other people, that ye should be mine.***

In Leviticus 20:24-26 that the children of Israel are so holy that they are separated from the other people (Gentiles) in the world. Also they are told to put a different between clean and unclean animals; this lets us know that they have a Holy dietary law to follow (Leviticus 11:1-47). The 12 Tribes are to be Holy for the Most High is Holy and he has severed them from other people that they should be his own.

Conclusion

The children of Israel are meant to be a light to the Gentiles so that they may also obtain salvation and the keeping of the law. The Hebrew Israelites are the Most High servant as a Nation and they are to do his will and walk righteously as he is righteous.

> ***2 Esdras 7:10-11 And I said, It is so, Lord. Then said he unto me, Even so also is Israel's portion.***

***11 Because for their sakes I made the world: and when Adam transgressed my statutes, then was decreed that now is done.** – Authorized KJV Apocrypha*

2 Esdras 6:55-56 All this have I spoken before thee, O Lord, because thou madest the world for our sakes

***56 As for the other people, which also come of Adam, thou hast said that they are nothing, but be like unto spittle: and hast likened the abundance of them unto a drop that falleth from a vessel.** – Authorized KJV Apocrypha*

They are so holy and precious that the world was made for the children of Israel sake. It's important that the Most High people walk, talk, and keep the Most High's ways, so they can store up good works in Heaven and show their Faith with works.

★ 20 ★

The Jewish People

The so called Jewish people over in Israel today who proclaim they are the real Jews are not, they are Khazars (white Europeans/Caucasians). I would like to also point out that they are High priest, sorcery, and wizards on a High level, they wear all Black from head to toe. They don't even believe in Jesus (yashaya) that can be pointed out in the Talmud (Jewish bible). They are from Esau descendants the brother of Jacob. Esau is the father of the white Edomites as I point in the previously chapter. Khazars are Japhetic in origin and converted to Judaism over the centuries. At that time Cordoba was the splendor of Moorish Spain (a mixture of black skinned Muslims and Israelites), and was the main center of European Culture. In his letter to Hasdai, King Joseph stated that he was from the line of Japheth, from the seed of Togarmah, and Japheth's grandson. He further stated that Togarmah, who was the brother of Ashkenaz, had ten sons and the Khazars represented the seventh son. With his own lips, this King had given the root of his being and the lineage of his offspring which was from the sons of Japheth. Here are the sons of Japheth:

Genesis 10:2-5 The sons of Japheth; Gomer, and Magog, and Madai, and Javan, and Tubal, and Meshech, and Tiras.

And the sons of Gomer; Ashkenaz, and Riphath, and Togarmah.

And the sons of Javan; Elishah, and Tarshish, Kittim, and Dodanim.

By these were the isles of the Gentiles divided in their lands; every one after his tongue, after their families, in their nations.

According to the King of the Khazars, his people descended from the family of Magog. Like all European nations at the time. However, ca. 740 C.E. King Bulan initiated the conversion of his kingdom to a new and different philosophy. Before the conversion, the Kagan invited representatives of Christianity, Islam and the Israelites to discuss the three doctrines. It was unanimously agreed, in response to the Kagan's question, that the doctrine of the Israelites was closest to the truth. And also in order for the Khzars to remain independent they chose the faith that neither the Christian or Muslims was part of but both respected. After the conversion the Khazar King changed his name to become King Obadiah. They displayed much hope but very little understanding, especially of spiritual matters. They had to invent their own brand of the law which later they named Judaism. The word "Judaism" cannot be found in the writings of the Prophets of old, neither is it found anywhere in the Holy Scriptures. Judaism is a misunderstanding or perversion of the customs of the ancient Israelites, as practiced by the Khazars. The edomites participated in the Roman War of 66-70 A.D. Arthur Koestler in his book "*THE THIRTEENTH TRIBE*" gives further detailed information about the Khazars and their conversion and how the majority of today's European Jews are direct descendants of them. The information contained in his book is backed up by scripture that shows the Jewish people over in Israel today are Gentiles, not natural born Hebrew Israelites. This is what he said:

> ***According to Microsoft Encarta, "Today, about 85% of all Jews are Ashkenazim". The Ashkenazi are not descendants of Israel, Ashkenaz was the grandson of Japheth and brother of Togarmah. Arthur Koestler further explains why today's Jews call themselves Ashkenazi even though they are the Physical seed of Togarmah.***

Aruthur Koestler shows that the Khazars took on the name of Ashkenaz because it was prophesied in the Holy Scriptures (Jeremiah 51:27). The Ashkenaz and their allies would conquer Babylon. This is what the Messiah had to say about them:

> ***Revelation 2:9 I know thy works, and tribulation, and poverty, (but thou art rich) and I know the blasphemy of them which say they are Jews, and are not, but are the synagogue of Satan.***

> ***Revelation 3:9 Behold, I will make them of the synagogue of Satan, which say they are Jews, and are not, but do lie; behold, I will make them to come and worship before thy feet, and to know that I have loved thee.***

The messiah said they are the synagogue of Satan. This lets us know that the real Jews are in poverty and in tribulation, and we can examine this by their condition today. Then it goes on to say, but they are rich, the real Jews are rich, they are rich spiritually and physically, but once they disobeyed the God of Israel they were stripped of their physical possessions. I agree with Arthur Koestler research. This is from page 17 of his book the "*The Thirteenth Tribe*":

> ***The large majority of surviving Jews in the world are of Eastern European descent—and thus perhaps mainly of Khazar origin. If so, this would mean that their ancestors came not from the Jordan but from the volga, not from***

Canaan but from the Caucasus, once believed to be the cradle of the Aryan race; and that genetically they are more closely related to the Hun, uigur, and Magyar tribes than to the seed of Abraham, Isaac, and Jacob.

The Israelites came from Canaan through the lineage of Abraham, Isaac and Jacob; while the Khazars came from the Caucasus through Gomer, Togarmah and Khazar, and the Edomites from Mount Seir through Abraham, Isaac and Esau or Edom.

Conclusion

The Hebrew Israelites descended from Jacob (Israel); while the Khazars descended from Japheth and the Edomites from Esau. The Israelites originated from northeastern Africa; while the Khazars originated from southeastern Europe and the Edomites from the southern Palestine/Jordan area. The Majority of Hebrew Israelites have black skin, according to the Holy Scripture, with woolly hair. The Israelis who are over in the land today have white skin, mostly blue eyes, long straight hair. The Hebrew Israelites (Jews) spoke Egyptian, Hebrew, Aramaic and later Greek, Roman, Spanish, various West African languages and today the various languages of the Americas. The Khazars (Israelis) spoke a language called Yiddish which many of them still speak still till this day. They are now in possession of the land known as Palestine. They (Khazars) have become known as the true biblical tribe over the centuries. The Jewish people over in the land today and around the world are being lied to. Allot of them are not even Jewish, they were put on films and other documents going into Israel to fulfill the prophecies. Allot of the Jewish people don't even believe in Judaism.

The Star Of David Deception

So what is the symbol known as the Star of David? It is the triangle that is the primary focus in all Illuminati realms, whether in the ritual ceremonies of the Rosicrucians and Masons or the witchcraft, astrological and black magic practices of other Illuminist followers. In almost every instance of occultism, the triangle is used among Satanists and witches, the double triangle, and the quote on quote Seal of Solomon, also called the hexagram, is reverence highly. This seal is actually composed of two triangles, superimposed on each other. The hexagram is one of the most powerful symbols of the occult, is used by witches to cast spells. Known more for being the Israeli symbol the Star of David—it is important to note that the Zionist organization adopted it as a symbol for the flag of Israel in 1897 which pre-dates its use in Freemasonry. Six triangles is the Egyptian hieroglyphic for the Land of the Spirits, in which this (6-pointed star) was the first sign or hieroglyphic of Amsu. In the Astro-Mythology of the Egyptians. The Zionism (Jewish Khazars) knew that in these end times that the chosen people (children of Israel/Jews) of the Most High that would wake up and come into the knowledge that they are the Chosen people of the living God. So upon our people waking up, they would run right back into worship of the idolatry they served while in bondage in Egypt, the Most High never gave the children of Israel a star to worship, neither to wear it around their necks as some due today. This can be pointed out in the Holy Bible:

> ***Amos 5:26 But ye have borne the tabernacle of your Moloch and Chiun your images, the star of your god, which ye made to yourselves.***

The Most High never gave the children of Israel a star, he gave them laws and statutes and commandments, and they themselves followed the heathens and made unto themselves a star unto a false god. They fell victim to the magical powers of this Star which was worshipped in Egypt, while they were wandering in the wilderness.

> ***Acts 7:43 Yea, ye took up the tabernacle of Moloch, and the star of your god Remphan, figures which ye made to worship them: and I will carry you away beyond Babylon.***

The children of Israel (Hebrew Israelites/Jews) worshiped this Star that was not given unto to them by the Most High. They took it upon themselves in disobedience to follow the gods of the heathens, therefore making them a Star unto their God to be worshipped. The Jewish (Khazars) people whom the Messiah identified as the synagogue of Satan, use this star and worship this false god they don't believe in the Most High, the God of Israel, they worship Satan. So the symbols they put forth is the representation of Satan, and by the chosen people upholding this pagan idolatry, they fail to come into the full understanding of the Most High.

★21★

Duty Of The Chosen People

The nation of Israel is known as the chosen people, but scholars and others never say what they are chosen to do. The bible is very clear about the job of Israel and the reason they were chosen. The Israelites are not the only ones to gain salvation (Romans 11:11), but it was and is their job to teach the world the truth about the heavenly father and his laws. This is why in Acts 10: the angel told Cornelius the Italian to go to Peter the Hebrew Israelite, so he might tell him what he ought to do. Peter taught Cornelius the full law of the God of Israel (Acts 10:33). The job of Israel is to teach the world the ways of the Most High. The children of Israel were given the oracle (word) of the Most High:

Romans 3:1-4 What advantage then hath the Jew? or what profit is there in circumcision?

Much every way: chiefly, because that unto them were committed the oracles of God.

For what if some did not believe? shall their unbelief make the faith of Ahaya without effect?

God forbid: yea, let God be true, but every man a liar; as it is written, that thou mightest be justified in thy saying and mightest overcome when thou art judged.

The children of Israel are the servants of the Most High and must do all of his services here on earth. One of those services is to go out into the world as priest and teach the other nations (Gentiles) about the Most High (AHAYAH). Some scholars are teachers would argue that the Most High cast away his people. I would like to say that isn't true. Israel is his servant and he has not casted away his people and they are to be a light to the Gentiles:

> **Isaiah 41:8-9 But thou, Israel, art my servant, Jacob whom I have chosen, the seed of Abraham my friend.**
>
> **9 Thou whom I have taken from the ends of the earth, and called thee from the chief men thereof, and said unto thee, Thou art my servant; I have chosen thee, and not cast thee away.**
>
> **Acts 13:47 For so hath the Lord commanded us, saying, I have set thee to be a light of the Gentiles, that thou shouldest be for salvation unto the ends of the earth.**
>
> **Romans 11:1-2 I say then, Hath God cast away his people? God forbid. For I also am an Israelite, of the seed of Abraham, of the tribe of Benjamin.**
>
> **2 God hath not cast away his people which he foreknew. Wot ye not what the scripture saith of Elias? how he maketh intercession to God against Israel, saying,**

Throughout biblical times and even now, Israel (12 Tribes) has become a spiritually dead people as I pointed in the previous chapters that they would discontinue from their heritage (Jeremiah 17:4). In the past and today, they have become accustomed to mixing the pure worship of the God of Israel (AHAYAH) with that of pagan idol gods (religion). In the process of doing this they continue to bring more curses down on them, and at the same time have lost the knowledge that the Most High has given them. Even at the second coming of the messiah, which is the times we are in, the end times, Israel will be used to bring the world into the truth. As it is written in:

> **Zechariah 8:23 Thus saith the LORD of hosts; In those days it shall come to pass, that ten men shall take hold out of all languages of the nations, even shall take hold of the skirt of him that is a Jew, saying, We will go with you: for we have heard that God is with you.**

All nations are going to come to the children of Israel because at this time the world will have knowledge of who they are and what their purpose. The children of Israel hold the keys of salvation.

Conclusion

The children of Israel are the only people who have been called the sons (children), servants, priest, chosen and the inheritance of the Most High. He never called any other group of people these things, but this doesn't mean that the other nations (Gentiles) are not welcome to have salvation; also the Gentiles are referred to as heathens, as written in these scriptures:

> ***2 Esdras 2:34-37 And therefore I say unto you, O ye heathen, that hear and understand, look for your Shepherd, he shall give you everlasting rest; for he is nigh at hand, that shall come in the end of the world.***

> ***Be ready to the reward of the kingdom, for the everlasting light shall shine upon you for evermore.***
>
> ***Flee the shadow of this world, receive the joyfulness of your glory: I testify my Saviour openly.***
>
> ***O receive the gift that is given you, and be glad, giving thanks unto him that hath led you to the heavenly kingdom.****— Authorized KJV Apocrypha*
>
> ***Romans 1:16 For I am not ashamed of the gospel of Christ: for it is the power of God unto salvation to everyone that believeth; to the Jew first, and also to the Greek.***

All people, of all languages and races are welcome to be partakers of the truth, and obtain the reward of everlasting life, But ALL that want truth and salvation must come to Israel to get that truth and salvation. For this is the whole duty of the children of Israel, is to be a light to the Gentiles as I stated.

REFLECTION NOTES

REFLECTION NOTES

REFLECTION NOTES

REFLECTION NOTES

REFLECTION NOTES

Bibliography

Equiano, Olaudah, and Robert J. Allison. *The interesting narrative of the life of Olaudah Equiano*. Boston: Bedford Books Of St. Martin's Press, 1995.

Koestler, Arthur. *The thirteenth tribe: the Khazar empire and its heritage*. New York: Random House, 1976.

Soukhanov, Anne H. *Encarta world English dictionary*. New York: St. Martin's Press, 1999.

Days of bondage autobiography of Friday Jones being a brief narrative of his trials and tribulations in slavery. Electronic ed. Chapel Hill, N.C.: Academic Affairs Library, University of North Carolina at Chapel Hill, 1999. Print.

The Holy Bible. Authorized King James Version Pure Cambridge Edition

KJV Apocrypha. Cambridge: Cambridge UP, 1983. Print.

Collins English Dictionary—Complete & Unabridged 10th Edition.

Charles, R. H. *The Ethiopic Version of the Hebrew Book of Jubilees: Edited from Four Manuscripts*. Oxford: Clarendon, 1895. Print.

The Holy Bible: New International Version, containing the Old Testament and the New Testament. (Textbook ed.). (1984). Grand Rapids, Mich.: Zondervan Bible.

Josephus, Flavius, and William Whiston. *The Works of Josephus: Complete and Unabridged.* New Updated ed. Peabody, Mass: Hendrickson, 1987. Print.

Lavey, Anton Szandor. *The Satanic Bible.* New York: Avon, 1969. Print.

The Temple of God, a discourse by Pastor Russell given at the 1913 covention of international Bible student. See (Pg. 120-125)

JEREMY G. SHORTER was born in Atlanta, Georgia, and lived in the inner city. He graduated from high school in 2008 and later started seeking work in the film industry. While out of school he started during research on his true heritage. In the course of his research, he has uncovered startling evidence indicating that his true heritage stems back to the ancient Biblical Hebrew Israelites. He later went on to create a website called, Israelites Unite, while researching, he found out about himself and his people. Later on he compiled all the research that he had from his site and decided to publish a book about his findings. He quoted from his book, "*My motive for writing this book is to enlighten the truth about the history and heritage of the so called Negroes of America and the 12 Tribes who are scattered throughout the world. Our true and rich heritage that has been hidden from us throughout generation to generation, which has been suppressed by the school system, religious intuitions, scholars, and many more to keep our people from knowing their true Nationality.*"

Mr. Shorter loves to teach his people who they really are so they can became and shine like that bright light that they are. For more information about his research and work, visit his website at: www.IsraelitesUnite.com.

www.ingramcontent.com/pod-product-compliance
Lightning Source LLC
Chambersburg PA
CBHW030446290526
45786CB00001B/469

* 9 7 8 1 5 2 4 6 7 3 6 2 8 *